Building
a Home
Full of Grace

Building a Home Full of Grace

John and Susan Yates

Baker Books

A Division of Baker Book House Co
Grand Rapids, Michigan 49516

© 2003 by John and Susan Yates

Published by Baker Books
a division of Baker Book House Company
P.O. Box 6287, Grand Rapids, MI 49516-6287
www.bakerbooks.com

Printed in the United States of America

Library of Congress Cataloging-in-Publication Data

Yates, John W., 1946–
    Building a home full of grace / John and Susan Yates.
        p.   cm.
    Includes bibliographical references.
    ISBN 0–8010–6415–5 (pbk.)
    1. Family—Religious life. 2. Family—Religious aspects—Christianity. I. Yates, Susan Alexander. II. Title.
    BV4526.3 .Y37 2003
    248.4—dc21   2002011683

Unless otherwise indicated, Scriptures are taken from the HOLY BIBLE, NEW INTERNATIONAL VERSION®. NIV®. Copyright © 1973, 1978, 1984 by International Bible Society. Used by permission of Zondervan. All rights reserved.

Scripture quotations identified KJV are from the King James Version of the Bible.

Contents

Foreword

I welcome and commend this book, which I encouraged the Yates family to write as a joint family effort. Since 1979 John Yates has been rector of The Falls Church (Episcopal) in Virginia, across the Potomac River from Washington, D.C. Its sizeable congregation includes many families. He and Susan have been married for over thirty years, and Susan has developed an effective ministry of writing and speaking, especially on marriage and the family. They have five children, who are now all in their twenties. Allison is married to Will, and mother of Caroline and Will Jr. John is married to Alysia and hopes to be ordained in the Episcopal Church. Christopher is settling into married life and graduate school with Christy. And Susy and Libby, twins, are both newly married.

I have known the Yates family personally for many years—John and Susan for about twenty, and their children since they were toddlers. I have stayed in their home and watched the family in its natural habitat. So I am able to testify from my own observation that this book presents an authentic picture of their family ideals, policies, and practices. One of the great strengths of the book is that every member of the family has had a share in writing it, has read it and endorsed it. So it is a genuine family product.

John and Susan Yates are familiar with the post-Christian culture of the West and interact with it sensitively, without surrendering to it uncritically. They have maintained their own Christian integrity.

Although their ideals of marriage, home, and family are high and holy, they acknowledge with honesty that they have not always attained them. They are frank and uninhibited in what they write, and the tone of their book is deeply serious, so that they often address their readers in direct speech. At the same time, they never lose their sense of humor over the absurdities of our human condition.

Building a Home Full of Grace contains so much practical wisdom, and is derived from such wide experience, that I do not think any parents could read it without learning valuable lessons from it.

John Stott
Summer 1999

Introduction
John

My wife, Susan, and I had been married for about a year. We loved each other dearly, but things were not going well. The level of frustration we had reached with each other was greater than any we had ever experienced. I was in graduate school, and Susan was working fulltime. We were trying to save money to buy our own home, thinking of having children, and working at establishing the habits necessary for building a mature relationship and meeting all of our responsibilities. Our families lived far away, and we were on our own.

We were fortunate in so many ways. We had loving families and close friends. But at that moment we were in the midst of an argument, and all we could think about was how incredibly selfish and stubborn the other was being. *How on earth could this person be so unreasonable?*

The argument escalated, and as it did, our sadness and disappointment grew until my wife exclaimed in utter frustration: "Maybe we shouldn't have gotten married in the first place. I don't think you'll ever understand me or what really is important to me in this marriage. Maybe we should just forget the whole thing. Maybe it's just not going to work."

Sooner or later nearly all married couples have an experience like ours. Couples may experience a combination of anger and disappointment, of hurt and resentment so great as to release a flood of fear and remorse that can cause them to doubt they will ever be able to understand or satisfy each other.

All of us want a loving, joyful, intimate family life. Perhaps you have glimpsed it, heard about it, or even been one of the very fortunate persons who has experienced it yourself. You may have confidence about how to build your own home into a strong and supportive family team, or you may be one for whom building a home that is truly happy and loving and is a shelter from the world's cruelties is a daunting challenge. All of us need guidance. We need encouragement and wisdom beyond our own experience to maintain a marriage relationship that is ever deepening and growing stronger while, at the same time, we are raising children to be joyful, thoughtful men and women who fulfill God's purpose for their own lives.

Children can produce their own set of frustrations in parents by wearing us down or wearing us out. For instance, it's the seventh night in a row that you have been up with your colicky baby, and you don't know how you can stand it another night. Or your three-year-old son or thirteen-year-old daughter has pushed you to the limit, defying you and disobeying you repeatedly until you find yourself having feelings toward this child that no parent ever wants to feel. You ask yourself, "How in the world did I ever get myself into this? Life used to be so much simpler."

At these painful points in family life, we need answers to tough questions, and we need a perspective that will see us through such moments. We will benefit if we have a sense of clarity about the long-range goals toward which we are heading. If we lack these foundational tools, we may give up and, in the end, miss out on some of the very richest of all of life's blessings.

We live in an age that has witnessed a dramatic pulling apart of families in America. At least 40 percent of children are not living with their biological fathers. Young men are confused about what it means to be a husband and father. Young women are perplexed about this question as well. It is a time in which those in families need not only guidance but grace as well, that quality we can receive abundantly through Jesus Christ. Because of grace, our failures to achieve the kind of family relationships we desire can become stepping stones toward a deeper, richer family life. Grace says, "I am with you for the long haul, even though we will repeatedly let each other down. Our love is not based on each other's performance. We do not give up on each other; instead, we keep on learning together, we forgive, we give each other the benefit of the doubt, and we look to God to help us grow."

There is no greater sweetness and joy in life than that of a full and loving home life. Few challenges are greater than those that will seem to block our progress as we seek to make our marriages work and as we try to raise our children in the way that is best.

Although there are no simple shortcuts in building a strong family, there are lessons to be learned along the way and godly principles, which, if followed, will guard us against many of the forces that seek to wound and destroy families. Two resources will help: biblical wisdom regarding family life and the experience of others who have successfully traveled the path before us. These resources will provide the perspective and hope many of us lack, but we must take the time to seek out this wisdom.

You probably long to have a happy, healthy, and truly Christian family. But perhaps your own upbringing did not adequately prepare you to shape the sort of home life you want. Your upbringing may have been unduly strict, or your family may have been fragmented and disconnected early on. You may have lacked the sense of closeness and security you desire for your own children. Perhaps you find it difficult to describe exactly what you are seeking in your own home life.

This is a book about families written by a family. In the chapters that follow, we lay out principles and practical suggestions for understanding and developing healthy family life built on the foundation of Jesus Christ. Susan and I have been married over thirty years and have five children, all married. Grandchildren have begun to arrive, and together the whole Yates clan is learning how to be family God's way. As you read this book you will see that various members of our family have had important input so that it is truly a family project. The chief author of each chapter is named at the outset of the chapter, but all family members have read and made comments on the manuscript. The stories we share are about real people, though sometimes a name may be changed or the facts slightly altered to protect anonymity. In the first chapter we look at what we mean by "family." Here we provide our family tree so that you can refer to it as you read our stories.

F. Ogburn Yates m. Sue Tucker   S. B. Alexander m. Frances

John William Yates, II m. Susan F. Alexander

| Allison A. Yates m. Will Gaskins | John W. Yates, III m. Alysia Ponzi | Christopher S. Yates m. Christy Borgman | Susy F. Yates m. Scott Anderson | Elizabeth (Libby) T. Yates m. McLean Wilson |

- Caroline
- Will Jr.
- John Tucker

I

What Is a Christian Family?

John

Since the creation of people, God's intention has been that all persons belong to a family. Marriage, home life, the nurture of children—these relationships and responsibilities are at the heart of all societies that even remotely resemble God's original design for humankind. Wanting to belong to a family is a natural desire God has put within us. Where two or more persons are bound together by marriage, by blood, or by adoption, you have family. Husband and wife, parent and child, brother and sister, uncle and niece, grandmother and grandson—all constitute a family. The family is God's original system wherein we are to be loved, protected, sheltered, fed, cultivated, and socialized. The strength and health of any society depends on the health and well-being of its families.

In the first three chapters of the Bible, we see that marriage and family relationships are foundational to God's plan for humankind. "God created man in his own image, in the image of God he created him; male and female, he created them" (Gen. 1:27). Men and women are equally important to God as partners working together for God's purposes. "God blessed them and said to them, 'Be fruitful and increase in number; fill the earth and subdue it'" (Gen. 1:28). Together men and women are to bear children, be family, and serve God as his vice-regents responsible for the well-being of the earth. This, according to God, is good, "very good," but for man to be alone is *not* good. "The LORD God said, 'It is not good for man to be alone. I will make a helper suitable for him'" (Gen. 2:18).

A person alone is incomplete—he or she needs community. Not everyone is called to marry, but we all have a need for a close, loving community. God's plan for most people is to find their deepest needs for community met within the covenant of marriage. In describing the woman as Adam's "helper," Scripture uses a wonderful word that means the wife is an equal partner with the husband, essential in the accomplishment of God's purposes. Husband and wife need each other to support, encourage, and balance one another. "Adam named his wife Eve, because she would become the mother of all the living" (Gen. 3:20). Bearing children and being family are understood from the outset of creation to be essential to the well-being of the creation. In the last half of the twentieth century, however, families in the Western world experienced terrific challenges. Divorce, unmarried couples living together and having children outside of marriage, single-parent homes, and a growing disregard for the values of traditional family life have resulted in widespread confusion and concern among persons wanting to marry and build strong families. The number of persons growing up in broken homes, wounded by a lack of security, and uncertain of what healthy families look like has grown enormously. Couples still fall in love and marry but are sincerely fearful of their ability to make the marriage work. Young men growing up without fathers have little idea about how to be wise, good husbands and fathers themselves.

Raising children has always been a daunting task, and if the home you grew up in was not secure, healthy, and loving, you somehow have to learn for yourself how to build your own family life. Not everyone is called to marry and have a family, but those who are *can* learn how to

14

build and nurture a strong marriage and family life. The principles are simple—they are rooted in Scripture and common sense—but they are not always easy to put into practice. We need God's help and wise advice every step of the way as well as the encouragement and modeling of others.

EXPRESSIONS OF FAMILY

There are three different expressions of family that are equally important for us to understand and appreciate if we are going to see family as God does.

1. The Nuclear Family

The nuclear family is what most Westerners think of as family—husband and wife or mother, father, and children. Creation was incomplete until God brought the first man and woman together and joined them in marriage. The first Bible stories are of this couple and their family life as they had children and weathered life's challenges together. From Genesis to Revelation, nuclear families figure prominently in God's purposes. The focus of this book is on this concept of family—parents and children living in close relationship with each other and with God.

2. The Extended Family

God's view of family goes much further, and to build our own families, we need to have a clear understanding of the broader picture of family life found in the Bible. In contrast to our typical view of the family as only parents and children, the Old Testament sees families not primarily as the small nuclear family unit, but the larger, broader family that consists of aunts, uncles, cousins, and the various generations that develop from one man and the family God gives him. We would call these our larger "kinship" circles. Jacob, for instance, whose name was changed by God to Israel, had a dozen sons, and their families were the forebears of the whole nation of Israel so that the Israelites saw themselves originally as one large family. As the people of Israel grew, twelve tribes developed that traced their origins back to the sons and grandsons of Jacob so that there became twelve large families. As they multiplied in number, different large families developed so that, for instance, Saul, the first king, described himself and his own wife and children as being of the tribe of Benjamin but of the family of Kish (Saul's father).

One's family, therefore, wasn't just one's mate and children or one's parents and siblings, but the larger extended family related by blood. I may have an aunt or a cousin here or there whom I'm not anxious to claim, but they are part of my family and I have a responsibility to know them, to pray for them, and to help them as I can. Today we gratefully look to many African, Asian, and Latin American communities to teach us what our extended family means in practice.

The different experiences of two friends of ours regarding their own extended families illustrate the way relationships with extended family can develop in different directions.

Our friend James has relatives scattered across the midwestern United States. Someone put out a call for a family reunion at the grandfather's old farmhouse, and James, his wife, sons, and four dozen or more others met for a weekend gathering. It wasn't a particularly happy time. The descendants of Grandfather Redding, who was an ordained minister, have chosen various pathways and philosophies of life. Although James and his family have continued in the Christian faith, most of the family members have turned their backs on the church. Most have prospered financially and socially, but several divorces— some quite ugly—and a couple of unusually bitter family feuds made conversation at the gathering somewhat superficial and at times tense. One couple was in mourning over a grandson who had died from a drug overdose. One granddaughter brought her lesbian lover to the gathering. There was a lot of conversation about investments, therapy, and the latest travel plans. One cousin had too much to drink, got nasty, and had to be restrained. James and his family found themselves more than disappointed that what they had hoped would be a gathering full of merriment and many happy shared memories turned out to be a sad affair.

Our friend Sarah and her husband and children recently returned from an all-day gathering with seventy or so relatives to celebrate her grandmother's eighty-fifth birthday. It was an uplifting reunion of four generations, all of whom still live in the same general region of the country. They were only able to be together for three or four hours, and no one wanted to leave at the party's end. Twenty or more family members gave speeches honoring the grandmother, some spontaneous and others prepared in advance. Family stories were told, some funny and some deeply moving. Even some poetry was read, and affection and appreciation were clearly in abundance. There was a strong sense of belonging to one another. Prayers of gratitude were offered and songs of praise to God were sung. As Sarah and her family began the long drive back home, they had a genuine sense of thankfulness to God for the privilege of belonging to this clan and a sense of hope for the future that this family would keep in communication and be supportive and loving toward one another however busy and widely dispersed they might become.

Although James's experience is becoming more and more common, the closeness and joy that Sarah's extended family has been able to maintain is what the Scriptures envision as God's intent for our wider family relationships.

If your own experience is more like that of James, take hope, because you can be the first of a new generation of healthy families. And if your experience is more like Sarah's, be grateful and passionately committed to working hard to maintain the strong family relationships that have historically characterized your family.

3. The Church Family

The most radical concept of family found in Scripture is presented in the New Testament. There we are taught that any two persons who are committed followers of Christ are family to one another. My neighbor Bill is also my brother, because he too has come to know and love Jesus Christ. We are brothers in Christ, and his son is "family" to me because he too is part of the family of Christ.

The most common form of address among the early disciples was "brother" and "sister." Over and over the apostle Paul addresses his readers as his brothers and sisters. This means my church is my broader family, and therefore we care for one another, share with one another, and help one another. Specific sections in the New Testament teach how to be a father or husband, or a mother or wife, but they are few and far between, because the instructions for Christian relationships also apply to our nuclear and extended families as well.

For instance, when Paul says we are to "carry each other's burdens" (Gal. 6:2), he is instructing Christians in their responsibilities, but he is also telling us how we are to relate to one another in our own homes. And just before Paul instructs wives to be submissive to their husbands (Eph. 5:22), he teaches that all believers are to submit to one another (Eph. 5:21). Thus, mutual submission between husband and wife is the norm for Christian couples even though the husband bears the responsibility Paul calls "headship" in the home.

Jesus greatly expanded our sense of family when he said that anyone who does the will of his heavenly Father is a mother or brother or sister to him (Matt. 12:46–50). The great truth inherent in this teaching is that no one need be without family—even if he or she is unmarried or orphaned or widowed. If we are followers of Christ, we are part of God's family. We are united in the Spirit even though we are not related by blood. It is clear that our first responsibility is to take care of our own flesh and blood (1 Tim. 5:8), but we are also called to do all we can for any who are in need in the church.

When my son purchased a new car, my dear friend Jerry taught him the basics of automobile care, because Jerry is more competent in those areas than I am. He was exercising his love and care for my son, a younger brother in the faith. When Sally and Bill's daughter Susie and her husband were struggling as newlyweds, I counseled and exhorted them in a way Susie's own parents were not able to do. I was exercising my responsibility to her as my younger sister in the faith. When my daughter went off to university, two other Christian couples gave her a computer, which we could not afford. In such practical ways we are family to one another.

We will be focusing on the nuclear family in this book, but we need to realize that God's family is broader and our own family is part of his much larger one.

WHAT IS A CHRISTIAN FAMILY?

Jesus said that wherever two or three are gathered, he is present in their midst (Matt. 18:20). In a sense, this is what we mean by a Christian family—a family that consciously has chosen to follow Jesus Christ, believing him to be the Son of God and Lord of the universe. A Christian family is the home in which the leaders seek to live their lives and shape the family values according to Christ's values as found in the Bible. The Christian family is not made up of perfect people and is not immune to problems. It may face sickness, sadness, poverty, and great needs. The difference is that Christ is at work and honored in the home. Here he is loved and worshiped. Christian family members may fall far short of Christ's example, displaying ugliness and even alienation. Many examples of discord can be seen even in the biblical stories of families God used mightily, but these bear the truth that this is not as it should be nor as it can be with God's help.

Family leaders have a deep desire to see the home become more and more a place in which Christ is pleased to dwell. They make a sincere and ongoing effort to ensure that every room in the house, every relationship in the family, and every activity in which family members are engaged is pleasing to Christ. Prayer, forgiveness, faith, and joy permeate this home. Here there is unconditional love and the conviction that God cares about every detail of the family's life.

Finally, the Christian family is not simply operating on its own, but is part of the larger Christian community, the church. God never intended that we attempt to build a marriage and family alone. The family that seeks to be faithful to Christ apart from the church will find the going difficult. In the local church we have four generations of Christian brothers and sisters, a community of friends who walk beside us and care about us from birth to death. If you have not yet found a good church to belong to, ask God to lead you to one, and begin seeking it out now.

SO WHAT *IS* DIFFERENT ABOUT A CHRISTIAN HOME?

Christian home life is radically different from that of families where love for God and the Word of God are not central. Where homes are built on Christ, three characteristics provide a sense of ongoing perspective and security. In the Christian home we (1) live in the light of eternity, (2) know that we are not alone, and (3) live together in the spirit of grace.

We Live in the Light of Eternity

God is eternal. This life is only temporary, but humans are eternal beings. God, in Christ, has promised everlasting life in heaven to those who put their faith in him. The temporary things of this life, which loom so large on our horizons now, are not really as important as they might seem. Persons who believe that life is limited to the here and now will put a much higher emphasis on things and on earthly experiences, while persons who believe this life is simply a prelude to eternity will be much more concerned with living now in such a way as to prepare for the next life. Thus, a Christian's values are determined by God's eternal values instead of society's values.

This world is only our temporary home. In light of this we will hold things of earth loosely, not looking to property or possessions for our sense of security. We will value infinitely more our relationships with God and with one another, because these will go on. Our children seem much younger than ourselves, but in light of eternity we are all very much at the same point. Each of us is only a beginner in the things of eternity, and we will go through eternity as brothers and sisters, not as parents and children.

Realizing that one's child or one's mate is an eternal being gives one a much greater sense of appreciation and patience and value. We do not expect perfection of one another now, for we are all simply children, just beginning life from God's perspective. This realization has a wonderful, radical way of equalizing all of us in the Christian home. It humbles us, encourages us, and gives us a sense of the long view in all matters. This brings to the Christian home gentle forbearance and hope. It is as though each of us wears a little sign that says, "I am an eternal being. I am infinitely valuable, yet please be patient with me because God is not finished with me yet."

We Are Not Alone

Because the Holy Spirit has taken up residence in every believer, no believer is alone. And Jesus taught that wherever two or three are gathered together in his name, he is in the very midst of them through the presence of his Holy Spirit alive in his people today. Therefore, we know that he dwells in each Christian home. Every relationship we enjoy in the Christian home is more than simply a horizontal one, because God is involved in every aspect of our life together. We are linked spiritually in the family as well as linked by blood.

The Holy Spirit is the great enabler who brings the supernatural powers of the almighty God into our lives personally. When Jesus walked the earth, he sometimes visited the homes of individuals and families.

His presence in a home made all the difference in the world. He brought such a sense of hopefulness that no sickness or sorrow could defeat those with whom he was present. Likewise, no problem need overwhelm us when the Son of God is near us. His presence still brings assurance to our homes today. Someone greater than ourselves is present to help us build our families. Jesus can still calm a storm and dismiss an evil, angry spirit. He can still bring peace into a troubled room.

When Jesus came into people's lives, he brought with him a clear sense of direction and truth. The Holy Spirit still exercises a teaching and directing ministry among us and will lead us as we seek his way. Prayer is crucially important in the Christian home, both as our means of seeking God's help and of asking his guidance. Prayer draws the family into unity, deepening the bonds of our union whenever we pray. We are never only dependent on our own resources, but always may draw from the limitless resources of our Father in heaven.

Whenever someone in the home opens his or her heart in true faith to Jesus Christ, Jesus comes into that person's home and begins to change the way family members see one another. In fact, Christians have the great and mysterious opportunity of treating one another as if Christ were in each of us.

Consider these mysterious statements:

You welcomed me as if I were an angel of God, as if I were Christ Jesus himself.

Galatians 4:14

He who receives you receives me.
Matthew 10:40

Whoever welcomes a little child like this in my name welcomes me.
Matthew 18:5

Whatever you did . . . you did for me.
Matthew 25:40

You yourselves are God's temple . . . God's Spirit lives in you.
1 Corinthians 3:16

Your body is a temple of the Holy Spirit, who is in you.

1 Corinthians 6:19

When Jesus Christ, by his Spirit, comes to dwell within us, our relationships in the home are radically transformed. If I am impatient or short with my children, in a sense I am being rude to Christ. If I lash out in anger and turn away from my mate, I am turning away from Christ himself. If I fail to listen, I am not listening to the Lord. When my child has a need or a problem, it is in a sense Jesus who needs my help. This tender and mysterious truth of the presence of Christ in our home can give us a whole new sense of holiness and wonder about our life together.

A Home Full of Grace

Perhaps the most precious word to the Christian is the word *grace*, which means God's free and unmerited favor. Our holy God is a just and righteous God. He has promised to punish wrongdoers and to right all wrongs in his time. Yet he is also a God of mercy. When sinful people come to him in repentance, faith, and true apology, he promises to withhold the punishment they deserve. Even more precious to us than mercy is God's grace, by which God not only forgives us our sins, but actually gives us many wonderful gifts we could never deserve.

In the Christian home we learn to live, not by law, and not even according to mercy, as precious as mercy is, but we learn as well, if we are wise, to live by grace. This means that we give one another love and attention, care and support whether we always deserve it or not. We are mutually committed regardless of one another's behavior on any given day. Whereas the atmosphere of many homes is negative and critical, the atmosphere of the Christian home is one of encouragement and graciousness.

Many adults find marriage difficult and family relationships threatening because they grew up in terribly critical homes. It was for this reason that Paul said, "Fathers, do not embitter your children, or they will become discouraged" (Col. 3:21). If we are overly critical, we run the risk of exasperating, discouraging, and alienating our children or our mate. They may just quit trying or become negative, angry, pessimistic, or very unsure of themselves. It will take much love, time, and patient encouragement to help them change.

In the home full of grace, forgiveness is always offered. Many families are tragically divided because someone hurt someone else and never asked for forgiveness. The New Testament calls us to "be kind and compassionate to one another, forgiving each other, just as in Christ God forgave you" (Eph. 4:32). True reconciliation cannot occur apart from repentance, but we do not withdraw our love even if the one who offended us has not apologized. Resentment will eat up a family if it is not replaced by forgiveness. We are always to be ready to forgive. Sometimes, however, we must practice tough love. To overlook a sin or harmful habit or attitude may be to become an enabler in someone else's life, allowing him to continue in destructive patterns that will harm both himself and others. Striking the proper balance is not always easy. We don't want to be enablers, but at the same time, we must always be forgiving. Home is the place where one should always be able to return without having to deserve it. A home full of grace is forgiving and, at the same time, is one in which we seek to draw out the best in one another.

The inhabitants of a Christian home are also patient and gracious. Courtesy and manners, kindness and patience are valued highly because they speak of grace. In such a home we are *for* one another, not against one another. Thus, it is a safe place to fail and to learn. We avoid negative words and attitudes, because we know that all are made in the image of God and are precious to him. Therefore, we watch our words, realizing that some things must never be said. We are like a team seeking to support, accept, believe in, and encourage one another to be the best we can be, even when we have failed one another many times.

Perhaps you did not grow up in a loving Christian family. Even so, you can begin to care for others in your own household and start a whole new chain of blessing and grace in your own family.

QUESTIONS FOR REFLECTION

1. What statement or Scripture mentioned in this chapter helps you in describing what is unique about the Christian family?

2. Describe a family you have known that has demonstrated these unique qualities. What aspects would you like to emulate in your own family?
3. Write out a prayer for your family based on your current dreams and hopes.

"Do not be afraid or terrified . . . for the Lord *your God goes with you; he will never leave you nor forsake you."*

Deuteronomy 31:6

2

Three Essential Commitments for Building the Christian Home

John with Susan

I f there were a basic curriculum for the Christian family, three foundational commitments would compose "homebuilding basics": commitment to the *covenant*, to *communication*, and to *cultivation*.

COMMITMENT TO THE COVENANT

At the heart of the Christian family is the marriage covenant. In every Christian wedding the participants are reminded that God established the bond and covenant of marriage at creation. A covenant is a solemn, sacred, permanent commitment between two people and before God. Jesus says of the marriage covenant, "What God has joined together, let man not separate" (Mark 10:9). Covenant is at the very heart of our Christian concept of family. God calls us into covenant with himself through Christ. He never stops loving us or giving to us. He says in effect, "I love you with an everlasting love . . . Never, no never will I forsake you" (see Deut. 31:6, 8; Jer. 31:3; Heb. 13:5). This is the example we are to follow in marriage. Our commitment to our mates is also to be every bit as strong and permanent as our commitment to our own parents and children. From Jesus' perspective, it was as unthinkable that a believing husband or wife would divorce as it was that a child would divorce himself from his parents. We are to honor and reverence marriage and always be faithful to our mate.

Every Sunday over a period of many years, the members of a church congregation in which we served observed a tall, handsome, and vital-looking man bringing his wife to church and wheeling her in and out in a wheelchair. She had gray hair and appeared to be a great deal older than her husband due to the ravages of a serious disease. When his wife had been stricken years before, this extremely successful attorney had immediately cut back his practice and made major alterations in his schedule to be sure that his wife was cared for. He came home every afternoon to be with his wife and to care for her through the dinner and evening hours. Her speech was halting and her attention was not easily focused, but her love and affection for her husband was as easy to discern as his equal devotion to her. In a day when husbands and wives break away from one another as frequently as they remain together, this example of long-term love and affection in the face of terrible adversity moved me deeply.

This couple knows more about love than most, because they have had to work out what love means in the face of disappointment and a distressing illness that has made life very difficult for them. It is because of the covenant of commitment this man made to his wife years ago that he has stayed beside her, even though she now can give him little in return for all he gives to her.

Christian marriage is based on the conviction that we are committed to one another in sickness or in health, in adversity or advantage, in good times or in bad, and in poverty or in riches. The commitment a husband and wife make to the covenant of marriage becomes a strong protective fortress surrounding the married couple and their children. This sacred vow made before God and our Christian friends in our church family exerts a kindly pressure on us to be decent and gentle and perse-vering in our marriage. It keeps us from pulling too far away from one another.

By the end of the twentieth century, numerous studies concluded that when parents separate and the home divides, the destructive impact on the children is felt for many, many years.[1] Anger, resentment, fear, and insecurity often result. These children have a harder time in life than those who come from "whole" families. They have a harder time mak-ing their own marriages work. They have adjustment and relational dif-ficulties that sometimes cause them to become so troubled as to end up impacting many others who must take responsibility for them.

Challenges to the Covenant

There are at least two major challenges to this commitment we make to the marriage covenant.

CHALLENGE #1: "IT JUST ISN'T WORKING—I GIVE UP."

A very serious challenge to the covenant of marriage arises when a couple comes to the point that their marriage relationship has deterio-rated and they conclude, "We have failed. There is no way to rebuild our relationship, so we will agree to quit." So commonplace is this con-clusion that many couples now enter into marriage not having com-mitted themselves to the covenant of marriage, but having signed a prenuptial contract. Contained in the contract are all the details describ-ing how, if the marriage does not work out, they will handle the disso-lution of their relationship. Certainly anyone who has experienced the tragedy and trauma of divorce would not want any of their loved ones to have to endure similar pain. It is understandable, therefore, that a man and a woman who have come from dysfunctional families might enter into such an agreement in hopes of avoiding more pain than nec-essary to themselves and their children if their marriage should break up. Nevertheless, the concept of a prenuptial agreement is displeasing to God, because it expresses from the outset an unhealthy fear that the marriage may fail and perhaps implies that there is not a complete com-mitment to the marriage relationship.

Certainly, there are tragic situations in which divorce seems to be the only solution. Nearly all of us have known others who have had such experiences. In these cases we thank God for his forgiveness and the ability to begin again. But Christian men and women who enter into marriage must get away from the idea that they will "just get out of it" if it doesn't work, because the covenant of marriage is the most solemn and sacred earthly commitment we will ever make.

The Bible tells us that "God hates divorce" (Mal. 2:16). And the wonderful, surprising truth is that, with the help of God, sick marriages can become healthy. Estranged husbands or wives can be reunited. If the husband and wife are both committed to the covenant and dedicated to seeking God's help and the help of others, they can rebuild their marriage. This is true because God wants to help rebuild broken homes.

CHALLENGE #2: THE DEMANDS AND TEMPTATIONS OF BUSY CAREERS

A second challenge to the marriage covenant is the idea that our careers must come first—although we would never put it quite so crassly. Still, many married persons believe that their own personal growth and development must take precedence over their marriage commitment. Many have careers that are demanding and gratifying. Many hold responsible positions that take most of their time. Their work is exhausting and can drain from them the ability or the will to give to their mates and children what they need to have a happy home. The home makes huge demands on us as well, and we don't always feel as appreciated at home as we may feel on the job. A husband, for instance, who is obsessed with his job and works very long hours, arrives home late only to find that his wife is frustrated because he hasn't taken care of this or that problem in the house. Or she is hurt because he didn't let her know he was going to be home late. She's feeling unappreciated and exhausted from being with the children, perhaps after having a full and challenging day at work herself. Often at home we are confronted with our own failures to be the kind of husband and father or wife and mother we need to be.

Few relish going home to that sort of environment, and therefore unconsciously work longer hours and spend less time at home. They develop their identity and seek their reward in their careers. The long-term result of such a process is not hard to imagine; it leads to family breakdown.

Some time ago I answered the telephone and recognized the voice of the daughter of some of our dearest friends. I could hear the distress in her voice as she was calling to tell us that her new marriage had collapsed.

Sandy said: "John, it has been terrible. So much of what I expected has just not happened. Charles seems too busy for me. He's obsessed with his job and surrounded by adoring younger people who think he is wonderful. He doesn't communicate with me. He doesn't understand why we need to spend time together. So many times he has hurt me by what he has said, and he seems to think that I am somehow different from the girl with whom he fell in love."

Apparently things had become so difficult that after many sad telephone conversations with her own parents, Sandy had left her husband and flown to be with them. Even worse, Charles didn't really seem to care. In fact, he even seemed to welcome her absence. After a period of separation she had decided to call me, because I had counseled and married them, and she thought perhaps I could offer her some advice.

As I listened, I realized this situation was very serious. These difficulties were not insurmountable, however, and were not so different from the challenges most young couples face sooner or later. It seemed that no one was urging Sandy and Charles to seek reconciliation. Sandy had been terribly hurt, and her friends couldn't bear the thought that she might be hurt even more before the process was over. My advice to Sandy was not, at first, very comforting. I told her to get on a plane, go back to Charles, and fight for this marriage with every ounce of strength she possessed. I challenged her not to quit no matter what he had done to her. They had too much going for them to throw it all away.

"The one thing that must not happen," I said to Sandy, "is for you to look back on this ten years from now and wonder if you gave up too soon, wonder if you gave your all to make this marriage work."

Some days later when I finally tracked down the young husband and asked for his side of the story, he said: "It just hasn't worked out. Sandy doesn't understand my needs or me. It must have just been a huge mistake to get married in the first place. We've had big problems since the beginning. What I want from her and what she wants from me are so far apart. It has been terrible. I work so hard, but she doesn't seem to appreciate it. You just don't understand how I feel."

"No, I'm sure I don't understand exactly how you feel," I said. "It sounds terribly hard, but think about this: Immature men make decisions based on how they feel; mature men make decisions based on what is right. You know in your heart what is right, but you have to decide whether you are going to keep on being a child and do what you *feel,* or if you are going to be a man and do what's *right.*"

This was, pure and simple, a test of two young persons' willingness to be faithful to the covenant of marriage. Were they going to *give up,* or were they going to *grow up?* Their love for one another was genuine, I believed, in spite of this current crisis. I was certain that with God's help and with the help of some wise, patient counselors, this couple could grow through this time, learn very important lessons, and possibly move into a whole new depth of relationship. But Charles had to realize that his relationship with his wife was more important than his job, and Sandy needed to learn to forgive him and believe that he could change.

It was some time before I heard from Sandy and Charles again. They moved, and I did not know how to contact them. Four or five months went by until early one morning I had a call. Both the young man and his wife were on the line, and I learned that with a broken heart but determination Sandy had indeed gone back to Charles to try again, and they were still together, reconciled, happy, and growing.

Charles said to me: "John, we just wanted to call you and thank you for the way you helped us last summer. You see, we're making it! We've been meeting with a minister, and he has greatly helped us. We're really happy. It's like we've got a whole new marriage now!"

Thinking back on that conversation, one thing Sandy said to me stands out: "If we had to go through all that pain and anger and hell last year in order for us to get to where we are now in our relationship, as awful as it was, I can honestly say I am thankful it all happened, and I'd go through it all again. We are closer and happier than I ever thought possible."

Rewards of the Covenant

If you are committed to the marriage covenant, you will be willing to go through whatever it takes to make your marriage work. Martin Luther described marriage as a school for character. Nothing reveals the cracks or strengths in one's character more quickly than the strains of married life, but with the exception of the parent-child relationship, no other relationship has such potential to mature us.

The covenant builds security. It forces us to deal with our problems, to work through them, and get things straight. It allows for mistakes and failures that most certainly will come in the marriage, but it provides room for us to keep on growing and working our way through these mistakes. No matter what may threaten the marriage, neither husband nor wife will allow it to sabotage their relationship.

Parental commitment to the marriage covenant also provides security for children and helps them to know that even though there may be times when their parents are upset with one another, they are bound together permanently. Children desperately need to know this about their parents. Surveys show that among the worst fears children have is the dread that something might cause their parents to divorce. This hovers like a heavy cloud over today's children and must be dispelled by parents reminding their children over and over again that they are married for keeps.

When our friends Sally and Ned have husband and wife arguments, they sometimes say to their kids: "We love Christ, and we love each other. We're not getting divorced; we're just having an argument. We will sort it out."

COMMITMENT TO COMMUNICATION

The second commitment that is foundational to healthy home life is good communication within the home, staying in touch with one another, keeping close. In most cases family breakdown can be traced back to communication breakdown—to a gradual loss of closeness between husband and wife. When conflict comes to a marriage, we are tempted to pull back from each other, nurse our own hurt feelings, and wait for the other to seek us out. This can lead to *emotional divorce*, two people living under the same roof but not connected with each other. The wife's feelings are hurt, and she tells herself: "It's too exhausting to try to explain what I feel. He doesn't understand and doesn't seem to hear me, so I just won't share my heart with him anymore. It's too painful, and it never seems to help. We'll live together, but I won't share deeply again. He can have his life, and I'll have mine." She begins down the path to emotional divorce.

But there is another path to take—the sometimes painful path to a deeper, more fulfilling marriage. It is the way of persistent communication, of deciding *again* not to give in to isolation, but instead to work through the hard times. We all will be tempted over and over again to take the path toward emotional divorce. Recognizing what is happening and then choosing to take the better path and work through the pain will lead to a deeper relationship.

Perhaps an even greater danger in marriage is not one faced in times of crisis, but rather the danger of gradually settling for a kind of superficial relationship with one another when things seem, on the surface, to be going well in the marriage. Subtly spouses begin to take one another for granted. We are busy with many things, and we conclude that we will work on deepening our marriage when things settle down. The trouble is, things never settle down, and apart from a commitment to deepening our relationship with one another, the marriage will begin to die rather than grow.

A marriage is like a house. If we do not invest a certain amount of time in the repair of our houses week in and week out, eventually they will fall down around us in disrepair. The roof leaks gradually become worse. The siding subtly fades. Termites quietly gnaw away on the foundations, and the house becomes weaker and weaker. A marriage is like that. We have to make a commitment to being constantly in touch with one another, or we will find one day that major problems have developed in our marriage that we simply had not realized. It will then be much harder to solve these problems.

Many couples make the mistake of working at their careers but expecting their marriages to simply fall into place only to realize one day that they are bored with their mates because they neglected to build the marriage through communication. Women generally realize the need for communication more than men do. A wise couple makes time to sit and listen to one another every day, talking not only about the developments and events of their daily lives, but also about their feelings and deeper concerns as well. This means making a priority of being together and talking when sometimes we would rather simply be resting on the couch or reading the newspaper.

COMMITMENT TO CULTIVATE A VISION FOR YOUR HOME

The third area of commitment fundamental to strong families is cultivating a vision for what you want your family to be like. The purpose of this book is to help you cultivate a vision and gain some tools for how to achieve that vision in your own home.

Married people, in the early days of establishing a family, have the opportunity to take some time to dream as a couple about how they want their family to look. One reason businesspeople are excited about their work is that they are pursuing an exciting vision for their business. We desperately need a sense of vision for our family as well. We need a sense of where we are going and what we are trying to accomplish. While God intends for all families to be characterized by love, nurturing, and encouragement, your family will take shape according to the purposes you envision for it.

As you begin to have children, you will realize that your children are quite different in terms of their gifts and personalities. The gifts, interests, and abilities God gives us should cause us to think carefully about how we want to build our family life and how we are going to help and encourage family members in growth and development. Children who are sensitive and artistic are going to have very different needs from children who are athletic and competitive. Parents need to dream together about their greatest desires for their children. What do you want your home life to be like? Do you want it to be full of laughter and activity? Do you want it to be a home that encourages creativity? Are peace and quiet a high priority, or do you like noise and laughter? Sports, games, certain skills, unusual interests, intellectual depth, gardening—what loves, what disciplines will you foster in your family? Do you want to expose your children to other people, to broaden them through travel? When you decide these sorts of things, they will help you gain a vision for your family.

Before my wife and I were married, we had the opportunity to spend some time with a wonderful family in the southern part of the United States. The music and laughter and love they shared for one another moved us deeply, and they became a model for us to reflect on as we married and began to have children. Spending time with families we admire can help us develop a vision for the sort of family we want to build.

Parents will need to determine what character traits they want to cultivate in their family and then plan ways to develop them. For example, to cultivate service to others, you will have to look for ways to direct your children in serving others and set an example so they can see the importance of this practice. When you put careful thought into cultivating a vision for your family, the result will be renewed enthusiasm for your family and a sense of mission and hope.

Commitment to your marriage covenant, to communication within your home, and to cultivating a vision for your family early on in your married life will provide you with an essential foundation for a strong family.

QUESTIONS FOR REFLECTION

1. How does the Christian concept of covenant contrast with the world's view of marriage?
2. What are several threats to the covenant of marriage in your particular culture?
3. What makes communication difficult for you? Determine one step that you will take this week to improve your own communication within your family.

"Seek first his kingdom and his righteousness,
and all these things will be given to you as well."
Matthew 6:33

3

Establishing
a Strong Marriage
John with Susan

When I was young I wanted quite badly to learn how to swim. The others in my family cared little for swimming, and I was left to my own devices to learn how. Thinking it would be easy, I jumped into the deepest part of our local municipal pool and started kicking my legs and swinging my arms as I had seen others do, only to find quickly that I could not keep my head above water.

Only God knows what would have happened to me that summer afternoon had it not been for an alert lifeguard who took note of my helplessness and jumped into the pool, pulling me quickly to safety. Not only had I tried to swim without knowing how, but I also soon realized that I did not even know how to tread water or float on the surface. Before you can learn to swim successfully in deep water, you need to know how to keep afloat and paddle around for an extended period of time. Similarly, in marriage and parenting there are certain basic lessons we need to learn that will keep us afloat, since much family life occurs in the deep waters of life—times when we feel as if we are about to drown.

Learning to be a good husband or wife and to be a wise and effective parent is like learning to swim long distances in deep water. If you are going to have a mature, loving, and truly good marriage and family life, you need to learn to "tread water" and "dog paddle" first. That is, you need a strong personal walk with God if you are going to be a good parent and loving marriage partner.

THE FOUNDATION: GROWING CLOSE TO GOD

The first priority in establishing a strong Christian marriage is one's own relationship with God—Father, Son, and Holy Spirit. God is looking for a growing love relationship with each of his children. When Jesus was asked what the foremost commandment was, his answer was very clear: "Love the Lord your God with all your heart, and with all your soul, and with all your mind" (Matt. 22:37). On another occasion when people crowded around and asked him, "What must we do to do the works God requires?" Jesus' answer was: "The work of God is this: to believe in the one he has sent" (John 6:28–29). As important as our relationship with our spouse is, it is secondary to our relationship to our Lord.

In his book *Knowing God,* J. I. Packer makes the following statement:

> What were we made for? To know God. What aim should we set ourselves in life? To know God. What is the "eternal life" that Jesus gives? Knowledge of God. "This is life eternal, that they might know thee, the only true God and Jesus Christ whom thou has sent" (John 17:3). What is the best thing in life, bringing more joy, delight and contentment than anything else? Knowledge of God. "Thus saith the Lord, let not the wise man glory in his wisdom, let not the mighty man glory in his might, let not the rich man glory in his riches; but let him that glorieth, glory in this, that he understandeth and knoweth me" (Jeremiah 9:23ff). What, of all the states God ever sees man in, gives him most pleasure? Knowledge of himself. "I desire . . . the knowledge of God more than burnt offerings, says God" (Hosea 6:6).[1]

In the Sermon on the Mount, the Lord stressed that our number one priority is to seek first the kingdom of God and his righteousness (Matt. 6:33). To seek first the kingdom of God means simply to let God be the King of your life. Then you will be equipped to become a mature and effective marriage partner and parent.

Many of us rule our own lives. When I am king of my life, my life is characterized by self-centeredness, anger, discouragement, anxiety, aimlessness, a critical spirit, and discouragement. I place my security in things or in other people. I evidence a lack of concern for others, a lack of faith, and little love for God. But when God is King of my life, I have an increasing sense of purposefulness, peacefulness, joy, and security. As I trust in God I experience humility and a deep desire to obey him. He helps me mature in character, in faith, and in godliness.

I must have a change of heart before God can become King of my life. I must believe that Christ is the Son of God and desire to know him better. I must acknowledge my failure to be all God would have me be and ask for forgiveness. And I must ask God to be the center of my life and guide me and help me to become the person he wants me to be. I learn to pray and let him speak to me through the Scriptures and through the Holy Spirit. As my relationship with him deepens, my life begins to change. Most of us do not change very quickly. The degree to which these new qualities of peace and godliness are experienced in one's life depends on the extent to which one is willing to trust God.

Scripture teaches us that God desires our prayers, our worship, and our attention through the study of his holy Word. If the president of the United States were to invite us to spend time with him, we would likely be quick to respond. How much more should we seek to make a top priority of setting aside time regularly to be with God in quiet times of prayer and meditation on his Word? Probably the most important activity we can carry out on behalf of our mate and children is to pray for them. In chapter 14 of this book we offer suggestions for how to pray for your family.

Putting Your Mate First

For the Christian, second only to our love for God is our responsibility to love our neighbor. We know that our neighbor is anyone whom we encounter, but as members of a family, our first and foremost neighbors are those in our own households. That we should love our mate and children comes as no surprise. But in this child-oriented age, it may be a surprise to learn that the relationship with our mate must take precedence over relationships with our children.

God's desire for the husband and wife relationship is nowhere expressed more beautifully than in Genesis 2:18–24.

> The LORD God said, "It is not good for the man to be alone. I will make a helper suitable for him."
>
> Now the LORD God had formed out of the ground all the beasts of the field and all the birds of the air. He brought them to the man to see what he would name them; and whatever the man called each living creature, that was its name. So the man gave names to all the livestock, the birds of the air and all the beasts of the field.
>
> But for Adam no suitable helper was found. So the LORD God caused the man to fall into a deep sleep; and while he was sleeping, he took one of the man's ribs and closed up the place with flesh. Then the LORD God made a woman from the rib he had taken out of the man, and he brought her to the man.
>
> > The man said, "This is now bone of my bones
> > and flesh of my flesh;
> > she shall be called 'woman,'
> > for she was taken out of man."
>
> For this reason a man will leave his father and mother and be united to his wife, and they will become one flesh.

The first thing God said was not good was that man was alone. None of the other creatures could satisfy the human longing for companionship; therefore, God created a companion for man to be a perfectly matched partner—a complement in every way. The rabbis used to teach that woman was made from the side of man to emphasize that she was always to be beside him and that they would face all that life would offer together as friends and partners.

"And God created man in his own image . . . male and female he created them" (Gen. 1:27). Equal in every way, they were to be loving, supportive partners. Later on God gave them children, but not until they had come into a deep commitment to one another. God never intended for our children to come between our mate and us. We are alone together as man and wife first before our children come, and then later on we are alone together again after they grow up and depart. We must learn as married couples to see our mate as our most important earthly friend and learn to strengthen that relationship so that it will remain strong always. Children will come and children will go, but the husband and wife remain.

A noted American physician, Dr. Alfred A. Nesser, of Emory University School of Medicine, has said:

> Parent-child relationships have been stressed so strongly for several decades that, for the sake of the child, husband-wife priorities are laid aside too easily. After the first child comes, a real test takes place. Will the mother now rob her husband of time and love for the sake of the child and ruin the relationship there, or will she continue to put priority on the husband-wife relationship? It is good to recall that marriage is permanent while parenthood is passing. Since marriage begins and ends with two, the primary concern is to keep that relationship in the best possible repair. Then, the parent-child relationship will take care of itself. Nothing is so central to a child's happiness and sense of worth as the love of father and mother for each other. There is no better way of giving a child a sense of significance than to see and to feel the closeness and commitment that the mother and father have.
>
> So parents should spend more time and effort in developing their own personalities and relationships. If father and mother are happy with each other, that contentment is conveyed to the child and not only results in good behavior and affection, but also a sense of personal worth. Children are not meant to be the center of the family. That center is the relationship of husband and wife.[2]

Five Basic Lessons

Every Christian couple must learn at least *five basic lessons* to build a strong marriage. The first is understanding the varied expectations we bring to marriage.

1. The Expectations We Bring

We all bring certain expectations to our marriage, which we believe if met will result in happiness and if unmet will lead to unhappiness.

Inevitably, your expectations will sometimes be in conflict with your mate's, so the sooner you can identify and explain your expectations to each other, the better you will understand each other. Failing to discuss personal expectations leads to an unsatisfying marriage. Some time ago the president of the Association of Family and Marriage Counselors in the United States said, "The most common cause of marriage problems is that partners' needs are in conflict but they can't discuss the conflict because they don't know one exists. They only know they are miserable."[3]

Listed here are some of the most common conscious expectations that individuals bring to marriage:

- a mate who will be devoted, loving, and exclusive
- someone with whom to grow and develop
- a constant support against the rest of the world; someone to stand by one's side in times of need
- companionship and insurance against loneliness
- a panacea for the strife and chaos in one's life
- readily available sex at any time
- a home that is a refuge from the world

Dr. Clifford Adams of Penn State University devised a test for married couples to help them articulate and better understand their own wants and needs in marriage.[4] He listed six ingredients of marriage in random order:

home and family
encouraging helpmate
security
companionship
sex
love and affection

Many thousands of couples ranked these ingredients individually in order of personal importance to them in their own expectations of marriage. They then ranked the ingredients in the order they thought their spouse would choose. The results were surprising. While women cherish love and affection as the most desired ingredient in marriage, men choose companionship. Most wives thought that their husbands would put sex at the top of the list, while most husbands thought home and family were of greatest importance to their wives. The actual preferences in order were as follows:

Men	Women
companionship	love and affection
sex	security
love and affection	companionship
home and family	home and family
encouraging helpmate	encouraging helpmate
security	sex

My wife and I had very different expectations of marriage as a young couple years ago. She seemed to expect me to understand her completely, sometimes without even telling me what was on her mind. She expected me to value time with her more than the time I spent at work. She expected that we would talk regularly and deeply of many things, including our own feelings and fears as well as our attitudes and opinions. I, on the other hand, was expecting someone who would always be quite easy to get along with and who would make few demands on me. I expected her always to be beautiful and eager for romance. I didn't expect to be challenged or confronted by my own failures and inadequacies. How little we knew of the realities of married life!

To build a strong, loving team relationship, couples must learn early on to express hopes and expectations of marriage and of one another and realize that most husbands and wives are coming from very different places.

2. Valuing Your Differences

The second basic lesson for a strong marriage is closely related to the first. Once you and your spouse begin to clearly articulate your expectations for marriage, you will see how very different you are. Valuing your differences is crucially important. Often two people are interested in each other because of their sameness, their shared worldview and experience. But over the years they remain interested in one another and deepen the relationship not so much because of their similarities, but because of their differences.

A major area in which we often differ from our spouse is in our perception of our own role in distinction to the role of our mate. The assumptions we bring into marriage are usually based on observation of our own parents, because they are, after all, more than anyone else the ones who demonstrated for us what a husband and father, wife and mother are to be like. They are our role models.

If you want to get some idea of what your marriage will be like, imagine, if you are the wife, your mother married to your husband's father; or, if you are the husband, your father married to your wife's mother. In so many ways you are your parent's child, and the way you view your role and responsibilities in marriage is based on what you observed in your parents.

Susan and I realized this vividly once years ago when I reached home at dinnertime and noticed that she seemed unusually cool toward me. I did a quick mental review of the day, remembering that we had been on good terms when I left in the morning, that I had checked in with her by telephone during the day, and as best I could recall, nothing had been wrong. There was no doubting, nonetheless, that something was indeed wrong now. Later in the evening I hesitantly approached the subject, asking if anything was amiss.

She looked at me as if I had rocks for brains and finally in great dismay said, "It's the dishwasher!" as though that perfectly explained the entire matter.

"The dishwasher?" I said.

"Yes," she answered. "All day long you knew that the dishwasher was broken. I told you this morning, and you haven't done a thing about it."

I've never been a particularly fast learner, and it was a while before the full significance of this revelation sank in. In pondering her statement, I said, "Well, I do remember now. Didn't you call the repairman? Didn't he show up?"

Now she was the one who was shocked. "Well, no, I didn't call the repairman. That's your job—you are the husband. You are the one who is supposed to take care of things like that."

As soon as she said this, I had a mental picture of my father-in-law, a wrench in one hand and a screwdriver in the other, working on a broken dishwasher. Then I thought of my own father in a similar circumstance, and at last I saw the root of the whole problem. I could never recall my father fixing anything around the home when I was a boy. If the oven was broken or some appliance needed fixing, my mother would always call a repairman. My wife's father was a true "Mr. Fix-it"; mine was not. It had not even occurred to me that my wife expected me to do something about the broken appliance.

Over and over again through the years we've had similar experiences that have shown us that we can become quite dissatisfied with one another because our expectations of one another in this or that situation are quite different. We assume that our mates will respond in a certain way, and when they don't, it confuses and sometimes angers us. Rather than being eaten up by anger, we should halt the conversation and ask, "Why are we having this difference of perspective?" Often our response needs to be simply laughter at the funny expectations we have. Humor dissolves tension and restores perspective.

I remember how irritated I used to become when our children were young because my wife's automobile was almost always a mess. Paper cups, school papers, cereal crumbs, half-eaten suckers, and an interesting assortment of other items littered the car. I found myself wondering, *Why in the world is her car always so messy? I don't remember my mother's car being such a mess when I was a kid. This is terrible!*

One day I realized that when I was young all my siblings were much older and my mother never had to deal with so many little ones at once. She also had someone to help her with cleaning the house and her car. I realized my wife, who had no help, was probably doing the best she could, and I decided that it was the least I could do to try to keep her car clean for her.

My wife told me after many years of marriage that it had been a huge disappointment to her that I was so often out of sorts and not fun to live with on Saturdays. Her dad had always been particularly cheerful and present among the family on Saturdays when the kids were out of school. But it gradually dawned on her that Saturday is a stressful day for me because I am feeling the pressure of always having to have a good sermon prepared for Sunday mornings. Realizing I was often preoccupied and irritable because I did not feel completely prepared for Sunday morning helped her to be more accepting of me.

It is important to remember that anger is not necessarily a bad thing in marriage and is often appropriate if it is directed at something that is wrong, so long as it is controlled and does not exhibit hatred or resent-ment. Anger can be an indicator to us that something is wrong, that something needs to be addressed. Too often we become angry because of misunderstanding or mistaken assumptions. On those occasions we can be greatly helped to know each other better *if* we choose to work through our anger toward a deeper understanding of each other.

3. Romance

The third key lesson couples need to learn to go deeper in their mar-riage is to maintain romance. Typically the husband rather than the wife will quickly settle into familiar and predictable patterns of relating with his wife, while the wife longs for him to court her and surprise her with fun things like he did when they were sweethearts. This point seems to be made in the Song of Songs. Listen as the king praises his wife for her beauty.

> How beautiful you are my darling!
> Oh, how beautiful!
> Your eyes . . .
> Your hair . . .
> Your teeth . . .
> Your lips are like a scarlet ribbon;
> your mouth is lovely.
> Your neck . . .
> Your two breasts . . .
> All beautiful you are, my darling;
> there is no flaw in you.
>
> You have stolen my heart . . .
> with one glance of your eyes . . .
> How delightful is your love . . .
> How much more pleasing is your love than wine,
> And the fragrance of your perfume than any spice!
> Your lips drop sweetness as the honeycomb, my bride;
> Milk and honey are under your tongue.
>
> 4:1–11

Some people find it hard to imagine such romantic expressions and sexual allusions in the Word of God. But such a deep romantic appreciation and responsiveness to one's spouse is very important to a good marriage. As husband and wife settle into their relationship, it is not uncommon for the man to become focused primarily on his work, while the wife's major concern is for her husband and children. This is usually true even if the wife has an occupation just as her husband does. Many men are content with a sort of business partnership with their wives, in which they see their wives as companions and bed partners. As long as the children and home are cared for, the meals provided, and he is satisfied in bed, many a husband is quite happy. For him romance is nice, but it's not necessary.

Such a superficial relationship is painful for most wives. They want something much more meaningful. They want to be loved, tenderly appreciated, and respected. A wife who does not receive these things from her husband will find it nearly impossible to communicate further her desire for romance. And when she tries, her husband too often misunderstands, thinking that an occasional box of candy or a bouquet of flowers is all she needs. What she wants is a little time with her husband, to be cared for, and to be told tenderly how precious and wonderful she is. She wants to be courted.

An Old Testament law established by God said, "If a man has recently married, he must not be sent to war or have any other duty laid on him. For one year he is to be free to stay at home and bring happiness to the wife he has married" (Deut. 24:5). This most certainly was one way of encouraging the growth of the Jewish people; it ensured that they would be fruitful and multiply. More than that, the law implies that the husband has a responsibility for the emotional well-being of his wife, and romance growing from time spent together is a vital element in this well-being.

Learning to focus on one's wife and not take her for granted during the early years of marriage is essential. Similarly, the wife is to live with her husband's needs and desires uppermost in her mind. (Read, for instance, Paul's teaching in Ephesians 5:21–33.) In our Western culture, as millions of wives have entered the marketplace over the last few decades, the result has been a great decrease in spousal togetherness. Thus, the more time the wife and mother spends working outside the home, the greater the need for romance in the marriage.

The Bible teaches that men are to cherish their wives and let them know they love them. The chairman of the Department of Psychiatry at Vanderbilt University School of Medicine in Nashville studied the place of affection in marriage. He particularly noted the importance of hugging and points out that in coming close to her husband, the wife is seeking a sense of closeness or of being protected and loved. She may not have any interest in sex but wants only to be hugged. Women are able to separate the desire to be held as an end in itself from the wish to be held as a prelude to sexual intimacy. This is harder for men, because touching and holding one's wife is much more likely to lead to sexual arousal. A wise woman will learn to say to her husband, "I just need to be held tonight." And a wise husband will understand that she is making an important request.

Deepening the romantic relationship means being in touch with each other and telling each other of your love. It means doing little deeds for each other that say, "I love you." It means taking the time to express unexpectedly your care for the other and making time to be alone and focus contentedly on each other.

4. Staying in Close Touch

A fourth crucial lesson most married couples need to learn is the importance of simply being together and talking regularly. Over the years various studies of the husband and wife relationship have revealed how little time married couples spend talking thoughtfully to one another. Unless we develop schedules that enable us to have regular, consistent, in-depth times of communication with each other, the romancing we have talked about will be shallow and meaningless. Breakdown in communication and loss of shared interests and goals are among the common reasons for broken marriages.

According to sociologists, there are two basic types of relationships between friends—primary relationships and secondary relationships. A primary relationship is an intimate bond in which two persons share their lives in a significant way. They have moved away from a superficial secondary relationship in which conversation is shallow and have entered into a relationship characterized by meaningful sharing, not only of information, but of thoughts, feelings, and concerns.

Primary relationships are vital, alive, and deep. Secondary relationships are shallow and functional. Mostly superficial communication takes place in such relationships. All too often in our family life spouses only see each other passing in the night or at quick meals between commitments. Loneliness, even among married people, is growing. For most of us life is very busy, and we have more to do than we can easily get done.

It is absolutely essential that we do not let our commitments rob us of significant family time together, and we can do this only by understanding that spending time together as husband and wife is just as important as anything else we must do. If there is little sharing of thoughts, hurts, hopes, decisions, and anxieties, then there is little relationship, and we become separated from one another.

Every week I enjoy getting together with eight or nine young men for breakfast, all of whom are in their early years of marriage. Each of them reports in turn the great challenge he is facing in finding time to talk and share deeply with his wife. Over the years Susan and I too have found that we are constantly facing this challenge of not having enough time together.

How then can we establish stronger patterns of communication in our marriages? I suggest three simple ideas. The first is to set aside one night a week as a "date night." Spending a lot of money on a fancy meal is not as important as getting a baby-sitter and getting out of the house for an evening alone. The idea is to spend a quiet, uneventful time just visiting with your mate, not only getting caught up on the day's activities, but also taking time to explore together some ideas, concerns, or dreams on which you don't normally have time to dwell. Some evenings when the kids were still young and at home, we would stay at home, charge the children with putting themselves to bed without interrupting us, build a fire in the fireplace, have a cozy dinner in the living room, and just enjoy one another.

Another idea is to plan regular escapes two or three times a year, away from home and children, for a night or two if possible, getting an especially good night's sleep and having a couple of days to enjoy each other with uninterrupted peace. If you find it difficult to get to a vacation spot, small hotel, or bed and breakfast in the country, perhaps you have friends who have a vacation cottage who would let you use it. Spending money on these times away is not frivolous; it is an investment in your marriage and will ultimately strengthen your family life.

For many years perhaps our most important tradition was what we called our "tea talks." This is my third suggestion for establishing stronger communication. During the week my wife and I were committed to a twenty-minute visit alone upon my arrival at the house in the evenings after work. My schedule often demanded that I be out during the evening, so we worked hard to maintain this appointment just prior to family dinner. It gave us each about ten minutes to talk about our day and our thoughts and feelings. The children were allowed to be in the room if they wanted to be, but they were not allowed to speak during this important time. When they realized they could not monopolize the conversation, they became bored and quickly left. Periodically we would try to broach deeper issues like, "How I am feeling about myself" or "How I am feeling about us" during these tea talks.

Those two topics were quite revealing for me, as I was never one to pay much attention to my feelings. Like many men, I was simply content to keep on moving, and I was seldom either "up" or "down." At least that's what I thought until one day, in sincerely trying to answer my wife's question as to how I felt about something, I began to realize that I was having some emotional ups and downs but had not been acknowledging them. There is something liberating about such a discovery, not just to oneself, but to one's mate, and our communication began to spiral upward significantly since we began to talk of deeper things during our tea talks.

People do not simply gel into the same position, keeping the same opinions and never having new feelings. All of us are constantly changing and are needing to share our heart and bare our soul with our mate, but often we shut one another off and don't grow together. Either we are close together in a marriage or we are apart; there is no neutral ground. We need to realize the great need for communication and initiate it.

5. A Shared Faith

A final basic lesson for building a strong marriage is that husbands and wives need a shared faith in God. A complete marriage is not simply a horizontal relationship; it is more like a triangle. The husband and wife are not only joined together, but, as individuals, are to be growing in the vertical direction with God. Few of us are strong enough to maintain a solid marriage today apart from God's help. He is the creator and designer of men and women and of marriage itself. He knows how to make marriage work. If you are consistently seeking God's guidance and help, you will have a better marriage. After all, he is *for* your marriage.

Christian couples have the opportunity to learn to pray together, not just in church and not just at meal times, although these are important. You and your spouse can experience a whole new realm of relationship by joining together in prayer at other times as well. When Susan and I were first married, we had both been in the habit of praying privately at bedtime. On the first night of our married life together, we agreed to close the day with an informal time of prayer before going to bed. This is not a time for lengthy and involved intercession, but simply a moment of thanksgiving and supplication on behalf of ourselves and our loved ones.

The by-product of this habit of coming together in prayer at bedtime is that it will enable you not to go to sleep angry with one another. You cannot pray well with someone with whom you are angry. If you're going to pray together, you're going to have to be reconciled first. Bedtime prayer has often helped Susan and me to experience reconciliation. It doesn't mean you solve the current problem immediately that night, but you come before the great Problem Solver together, asking for his help. It is not realistic to think that you will always be able to forgive and forget one another's faults or hurtful words quickly and easily, but the commitment to pray together ensures that you end the day without grudges, having taken all steps possible to see that your relationship is right, both with one another and with God.

Couples can begin by saying a blessing at meals or by holding hands and saying the Lord's Prayer or by joining in certain prayers of the church. As you become more comfortable with praying this way, it becomes easier to formulate your own personal prayers together. It is best to pray aloud, because it enables your mate to share in your prayers. The Book of Ecclesiastes pictures this relationship in these lovely words:

> Two are better than one,
>   because they have a good return for their work:
> If one falls down,
>   his friend can help him up.
> But pity the man who falls
>   and has no one to help him up!
> Also, if two lie down together, they will keep warm.
>   But how can one keep warm alone?
> Though one may be overpowered,

two can defend themselves.
A cord of three strands is not quickly broken.

4:9–12

This is a picture of a marriage in Christ. The threefold strands are a husband and wife whose lives have been intertwined with that of God. Two are better than one, but three is better than two when the third strand is the Lord. The little diagram below illustrates the basic truth that the closer you grow to God, individually, the closer you grow to one another.

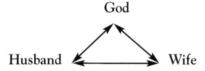

QUESTIONS FOR REFLECTION

1. What statement or Scripture reference that you read struck you as particularly important in your own life? What might God want you to learn from this?
2. What are some of the ways in which you and your mate are different? How can these differences be complementary rather than devisive?
3. Begin each day by thanking God for one specific trait in your spouse that you appreciate.

Two are better than one,
because they have a good return for their work:
if one falls down
his friend can help him up.

Ecclesiastes 4:9–10

4

The Seasons
of Family Life
Susan

One of our daughters telephoned us a while ago while at school. She was feeling tired, bored, and useless at this point in her university career. "Maybe I should just quit school and do something more worthwhile," she sighed.

She reminded me of her older brother, who just two or three years before that had been feeling exactly the same way. He weathered that particular crisis, persevered, and completed his schooling with a high degree of satisfaction and achievement. Now he is in another season of life, working in the business world and newly married. His new season seems much more exciting than the one his sister is in. One thing is sure: We all go through different seasons in life, some much more difficult than others, but all full of great challenges and significant rewards if we have the eyes to see them.

Some seasons seem longer than others. When the children were all small, during one month-long period we had three cases of chicken pox, two ear infections, one case of bronchitis, and three bouts of the flu. We thought we might perish from nursing sick children and wondered what it would be like if all the family were healthy again at the same time.

Whatever stage of life we are in, we need to learn that many of the difficulties we experience are temporary. They are usually normal and will eventually change with the passage of the particular season we are in.

In each season we are likely to experience frustrations. A new mother may feel resentment at the demands being made on her time by her baby, the same baby she longed for and prayed for. A teenager struggling to be accepted often thinks he is the only one who feels awkward and out of place. It's common to feel alone during the challenges of a particular season.

During these periods we tend to enlarge small problems and see them as major crises. This child will *never* become potty trained, and I will be changing his diapers when he is six years old! How will my son *ever* get into a good college with his dismal academic performance? We may feel as if things only get worse and never get better. In times like this we lose perspective on our situation. But when the season passes and we look back, many of the things that seemed so crucial really weren't, given the perspective of time and experience. This is why it is helpful to have friends who are older and have lived through a few more seasons than we have.

It is also helpful to try to see things from God's perspective. Wherever you are in life, God is in control. He is our rock and our fortress (Ps. 31:2–3). His love and presence are constant. He will also lead and guide us. Sometimes we have to turn away from the challenges at hand and simply look to God for comfort and peace. He has a purpose and plan for every phase of our life, and he is the master of what happens. He has called us to be exactly where we are and will teach us in each season. "I will instruct you and teach you in the way you should go; I will counsel you and watch over you" (Ps. 32:8). Ask God what he would teach you in this season you are in right now. When we develop a sense of hopeful expectancy, looking to learn from God in each season of life, we will be more open to his gently teaching us about himself and how he works.

As we walk through these different times in our lives, God longs to give us the resources to enjoy them. We are not meant only to endure toddlers or teenagers, but to rejoice in them, even though there are certainly times when all we can do is hold out until the end of the day.

THE EARLY YEARS TOGETHER

As we have already discussed, newlyweds have many adjustments. The first few years of marriage are a season of leaving your parents, or, if you're older, losing your independence and establishing oneness. It can be awkward and it can be delightful. You need a sense of humor to see this season as a time of realizing how you and your spouse are different and how you are alike, how your expectations must change and how you can become one.

When the wife is pregnant, both spouses are affected but in different ways. Some women feel wonderful and seem to glow, while many are sick and feel terrible. I remember when I was pregnant, driving down the street with two toddlers and having to stop the car, open the door, and throw up. Pregnancy also can make us act out of character. It was best for me not to make many important decisions during this season when I was tired and my emotions weren't trustworthy. Husbands sometimes act out of character too and may worry inordinately, particularly when the first child is on the way. One friend of ours completely lost his hair during his wife's pregnancy because of his fears and uncertainties about his ability to be a good father and about the health of his wife and child.

Once the first baby does arrive, we find we have entered into a new season overnight, and we wonder how one small being can bring about so many immediate changes. No matter how carefully we have organized our lives, once children begin to come, it's like starting all over again. If the wife has given up her job to be at home full time with the child, she has to adjust to being at home, which is quite hard for some yet exciting and liberating for others. If she is still working, she has to learn to balance the needs of another person in the home, which involves more planning and more sacrifice on the part of both parents. I thought our first child was the hardest, because I went from having great freedom to feeling really tied down.

Of course the joy of this season is unlike anything we have experienced as we lovingly hold our babies and gain a whole new understanding of how God our Father adores us. Our parental emotions are a wonderful taste of what God's love for us must be like. As we observe the amazing growth of these little persons, we realize that they experience a great sense of wonder as they look around themselves in awe, taking in sunlight and colors. This reminds us of how much wonder we can experience in life as we recognize all that God has done for us. As we see the world through an infant's eyes, we have a great opportunity to recapture the wonder and appreciate the beauty around us that we perhaps have taken for granted.

THE TODDLER YEARS

The toddler years are the most trying and the most precious. Energetic children constantly exhaust their parents, yet they also delight us with their unpredictable actions and responses. Three unique challenges face us during this time: *teaching obedience, harnessing energy,* and *maintaining control.*

Between the ages of two and three the battle of the wills rages continually, because it's the season during which the child seeks to determine who is in control. Training a child to obey is an exhausting challenge. Along with this comes the challenge of harnessing the toddler's great energy. Toddlers don't learn just to walk, they learn to run; and they seem to prefer that pace. This is not the time to redecorate your house; rather, it's the time to strip things down, to lock cabinets, and to ensure that the children can't get into anything that will harm them. Toddlers make mothers feel that they've lost control of their families. They constantly interrupt, they are unpredictable, and they give orders incessantly.

A mother of toddlers certainly has to lower her expectations of what she can accomplish in a day. But she also has much to enjoy during this season as she observes the interesting and humorous things children do and say. It's wise to write down the funny things children say during this time. I remember when Libby saw the ocean for the first time. Her wide eyes held a glint of amazement and fear. "Mommy," she exclaimed, "it's too full. You need to let some of it out." I quickly wrote this down, because it was so precious I didn't want to forget it. Take funny photographs—the child covered with mud, a game of dress-up in old clothes, a face covered with cereal. Later you and your child will laugh more at these and enjoy them more than photos of the family in their best dress. When you're in the midst of the toddler years, it seems they will never pass, but this season does pass quickly, and sometimes parents look back wishing they had taken more time to enjoy their little ones. When you're surrounded by whining children and dirty diapers, you long for the time to end. When they leave for school, you wonder how time passed by so quickly, and you find yourself longing for some of those toddler antics.

AS THE KIDS MATURE

During the school years new and different challenges present themselves. Whereas during the toddler years parents find themselves physically worn out from chasing little ones, parents of teens and preteens are more likely to experience emotional exhaustion. One child is shy and hesitant, while another is the life of the party. One is longing for friends, and another has too many. Children have different needs, and it's easy to feel overwhelmed as we attempt to meet all these needs.

During the teen years, children become increasingly independent. As we train and guide them, we have to remember to encourage them gradually toward independence. This involves their learning personal responsibility, making wise decisions, and carrying through on commitments.

Teaching children to make wise choices is a crucial challenge during these years. Active older children have many opportunities and want to do everything. One wants to play on two or three athletic teams at the same time. Another wants to be in choir and take ballet lessons. Parents sometimes feel overwhelmed by these opportunities and desires.

Along with the challenges of growing independence and making wise choices comes the difficulty of learning to help our preteens and teens maintain a positive self-image. A child's self-identity is a fragile thing, and peer pressure can be powerful. Wise parents stay close to their children, listening and observing carefully. During this period parents have the unique opportunity to point them to God as the one who must meet their needs. These are the years when children can learn to pray about decisions they must make and to take their loneliness and sadness to God and find companionship with him. This is not the time to spend less time with our children. Just being around them during these years is crucial in order to understand what's going on in their lives. Some families find it necessary to send their children away to boarding school, and this makes the challenge of staying close to the children all the more difficult, but it is no less important during these formative years.

Some good friends of ours moved to another town when their children were adolescents. This couple loved to entertain and were always social leaders in our community. But when they moved, they made a decision not to get as involved in social activities, deciding rather that since their kids would be home only a few more years, they would spend most of their weekend time doing things together as a family. They realized there were many years ahead when the kids would be grown and gone during which they could become more involved again socially. Now, many years later, they have close relationships with all their adult children because of the time they invested during their youth.

Maturity comes as we learn to postpone to another season something that we would like to do now. We have to learn to wait. It isn't easy, but it is wise. It is helpful to ask, "Am I doing something now that I might be better off postponing?" Our children will have to learn this same lesson, and they will learn as they watch us.

BEING ALONE AGAIN

As the children grow up and leave home, we enter a season of letting go. This can be especially hard on the mother, particularly if she has put her whole life into her children. From the time the children are small, women need to be preparing themselves for when their children will leave. Dream about your next career after your children, sharpen your skills, consider part-time work, or take a class. If a couple begins this process before the children leave, the adjustment to the empty nest will be much easier.

John and I feel personally that if a mother can be at home when the children are still at home, that is best. If it is necessary for the mother to work, perhaps she can arrange her hours to be at work only when the kids are away from the house. When the kids come home after being at school, it makes a big difference to have Mom there to listen and comfort, to carpool to all those extracurricular activities, and to be a friend. It is certainly not always possible, but the more it can be done, the better.

Parents often find it emotionally difficult to let go of their children. As we study the life of the holy family in the New Testament, we realize from the few brief words about Mary, the mother of Jesus, how hard this lesson was for her to learn. We have to learn how to stay deeply involved in our children's lives, loving and counseling, but allowing them to make many of their own decisions. Some parents go too far and leave all decisions in their children's hands when they leave for university or when they first leave home. Older teenagers still need our guidance, and it's sometimes tricky to know when to step in and when to hold off and let them make mistakes. This demands prayer and thoughtful effort on the part of the parents.

Sometimes grown kids leave and then, for various reasons, come back home again. This is a challenging situation for parents, because the kids have become accustomed to living on their own.

Once the children are grown, parents have the freedom to choose options they have not had before, and this is a time to pursue, as individuals and as couples, interests that have been postponed. This is also a time for solitude.

WHEN THE SEASONS OVERLAP

Most of us will not be exclusively in one season but will find ourselves coping with children of different ages at the same time. Friends of ours have four children whose ages span fourteen years. They say that one of the biggest challenges of overlapping seasons has been shifting gears mentally, learning how to switch from working with one child on a college application to teaching another how to ride a bicycle. Older children can gain great training for being parents if they have young siblings, and it's fun for parents with older children to share with them in the joy of watching the amusing antics of the smaller ones. Older children provide models and examples for younger siblings, and this can be a great blessing during the overlapping seasons.

Some will find themselves grappling with challenges in the lives of their own parents while their children are still at home. The way we love and care for our parents through the years is another way in which we train our children and will determine how they relate to us when they are grown and we are in our declining years. Our children will learn to honor us as they observe us honor our parents. If we criticize or neglect our parents, our children will be more likely to treat us in the same manner one day. But if we sacrifice and reach out to our aging parents, we provide a model of caring that our own children will not miss.

When the seasons overlap and we find ourselves facing a great range of demands, we need to remind ourselves that God is still in control and that he will bring us through this time. Nothing during these mixed-up times need be wasted. If we can see our lives in seasons, it will enable us to gain perspective and keep the positives and the negatives in balance. If we can relax and enjoy the unique blessings of the particular season we are in rather than longing for the next one to come, we will experience God's faithfulness more fully in the present.

QUESTIONS FOR REFLECTION

1. How is the concept of "seasons in life" helpful to you?
2. What are some of the challenges and blessings of your current season in life?
3. What is God teaching you about himself during this season? Meditate on Psalm 46.

The LORD your God is with you,
he is mighty to save.
He will take great delight in you,
he will quiet you with his love,
he will rejoice over you with singing.

Zephaniah 3:17

5

The First Child
Allison with Will

My husband, Will, and I remember the day we discovered we were expecting our first child. We were on vacation in Southern California, staying in a bed and breakfast with very thin walls. The bathroom, where I took a home pregnancy test, was all the way down the hall from our room. In a state of shock over what appeared to be a positive result, I crept down the hall to our room. In a hushed voice so as not to disturb any other guests, I showed the test to Will and said, "Do you see what I see?" Tremors reached my toes as we both agreed that it appeared to indicate I was indeed pregnant. Then, with a shudder and a sigh, my dear husband threw himself on the bed and stopped speaking—not exactly the reaction I had been expecting. I was hoping that we would begin discussing baby names with joyful anticipation and then run out to the nearest bookstore and stock up on the "classics" of pregnancy and child-rearing books. Instead, the rest of our vacation was clouded by an inexplicable weight. My husband virtually "shut down," while I went from excited anticipation to worrying that I had inadvertently done something to harm the baby before I had realized I was pregnant. I wanted to talk about the baby and the changes he or she would bring. My husband didn't want to discuss it. I couldn't understand his reaction at all. We had been talking about starting a family for several months and had been hoping that I would become pregnant. But somehow talking about the matter and actually having it happen were two vastly different things. Neither of us knew quite what to do.

It wasn't until several months later that we realized our different reactions to the news that Baby was on the way were quite normal. My husband was greatly reassured to read that grief is one of the most typical reactions men experience at the news of an upcoming child.[1] I was looking forward to the start of my "new life" of motherhood—I saw it as God's calling in my life. Will, however, was feeling as if any ounce of freedom he had once possessed was disappearing before his very eyes. Not only would he have a wife to support, but a child as well. And one child would probably lead to two, three, four—as we had always talked of having a large family. Gone were the days when we could go to a late movie on the spur of the moment, take weekend trips with our friends, or play recreational sports. Every ounce of time, energy, and money would be devoured by this new addition to the family. Life as we had known it was over—and we were only twenty-five!

Thankfully, as the time drew nearer for the arrival of our child, my husband grew more and more excited. We got a puppy, and falling in love with the dog was such a delight for Will that he realized a child could only be better. In talking with other friends who had children of their own, we both came to understand that life as we knew it was indeed over, but that life as parents was a rich and joyful experience we would love more than we ever dreamed. We agreed that we would have to work all the more diligently to allow space for "fun" in our lives and not let parenthood take over our very selves. We started to prepare for the big day.

CONTEMPLATING PARENTHOOD

As young couples beginning their life journey together, we all face the same questions relating to parenthood. Probably the first and most obvious question you will have discussed before you even marry is the issue of family planning. Thoughtful Christians are not in agreement about the use of contraceptives. Most feel that it is sensible to become as familiar as possible with the woman's ovulation cycle and to avoid intercourse during the fertile period to prevent conception until the couple are ready to become parents. Others believe that, especially during the early years of marriage, it is sensible to use contraceptives that are safe and recommended by a physician. Christians universally condemn abortion as a form of birth control. It is one thing to take precautions to avoid pregnancy yet quite another to destroy a young life that God has already created. Our family strongly believes that once a child is conceived, whether "planned" or not, we are gratefully and graciously to accept this child as God's precious gift.

Another question is, "Do we want to have children at some point?" followed by "When?" and "How many?" Some couples haven't fully addressed these questions when they discover a "honeymoon baby" is already on the way. Or some may find becoming pregnant difficult or impossible and need to seek special medical advice or other options. Some may choose to pursue fertility treatments, while others may elect to adopt. Each couple will approach these questions and situations differently, but there are some common themes that will be helpful for any couple considering parenthood.

When we ask, "Should we have children?" we need to remember that God is in control. Ultimately, this decision is up to him. He is gracious to give us free will in directing most areas of our lives, but in all things we must surrender to his lordship. This is especially true as we approach parenthood. In Deuteronomy we are told, "Love the LORD your God with all your heart and with all your soul and with all your strength" (6:5). We must agree before God that he is Lord of our lives and our marriage, and that we seek only his best for us. We can have confidence that whatever his plan is, is best. Jeremiah 29:11–13 reminds us of this clearly, as God promises: "I know the plans I have for you . . . plans to prosper you and not to harm you, plans to give you hope and a future. Then you will call upon me and come and pray to me and I will listen to you. You will seek me and find me when you seek me with all your heart." God's plan is for our good, and part of that plan is drawing us nearer to him as we seek his heart in the processes of life.

We must also have a clear understanding of what it means to be a family. We discussed the nature of a Christian family at length in chapter 1. In the biblical story of creation, God completed Adam by bringing him a wife. God did not give Eve to Adam along with four children! In fact, children did not come until after Adam and Eve had been banished from Eden. In the eyes of God, husband and wife bound together in the Holy Spirit make the family unit whole. Marriage, this cleaving together of one another before God, is the foundation of all family life. The addition of children is a gift from the Lord that may come later—but family begins with just two people.

Understanding this concept of a family is essential for several reasons. If you have children, you will need to constantly rely on your personal relationship with God as well as the foundational relationship of husband and wife to function as godly parents. Once children have arrived, spouses must fight the natural tendency to make them the focus of the family. Children must not become the center, to the detriment of Mom and Dad's marriage, or the entire family will be out of balance and discord will result. Moreover, if, for whatever reason, you decide not to have children, or if you are prevented from doing so by circumstances beyond your control, you will need the assurance that you are still complete in God's eyes, as individuals and as mates.

Assuming that children are part of God's plan for your life, a second practical question arises: When should you have them? How will you know when you are ready? The answer will depend on each individual situation. As a general principle, you must be whole in God before you seek to add children to the picture. Children will not fill up the empty spaces in your heart or your marriage. Only the Lord can do that. Children will not draw a struggling couple together. Many unfortunate couples mistakenly decide, "We're having trouble in our marriage. Let's have a baby—that will surely draw us closer together!" Children may kindle a certain closeness between husband and wife—but they will also drive a wedge between you if you are not already cleaving to one another as if your life depended on it.

ISSUES TO CONSIDER

Let us offer a few practical suggestions for deciding when you are "ready."

1. *Understand that you will never be completely ready.* You will never be smart enough, rich enough, or experienced enough to have children. You have to learn as you go, so don't think that one day you will simply know that it's time to begin. Adam and Eve probably didn't know what the command to "be fruitful and multiply" was all about until Eve became pregnant. The Bible doesn't mention it, but you can bet they were surprised with what came next.

2. As much as your circumstances allow (this will depend on your chosen method of family planning), *give yourselves time to cleave together as man and wife before you bring children into the picture.* Rushing into pregnancy in the first year of marriage is not generally advisable, because there are so many other adjustments to face.

3. *Develop and stick to a family budget before you have children.* Being able to manage your family finances wisely is vitally important when there are just two of you. Budgeting only gets more complicated with additional mouths to feed, bodies to clothe, and so on. This is not to say that you must wait until you "have enough money" to have children. You might never have them if you wait for that golden moment! But it is advisable to be as debt-free as possible before your family begins to expand. Furthermore, you should decide if one of you will be at home full time with the children, as this will most likely involve giving up an income.

4. *Talk about it!* Spend hours sharing about your own families—what you enjoyed about your growing up years, what you would change for your own children. Understand what your mate thinks about having children. For many couples today, this is an area of pain. Your family may have been broken by divorce, unfaithfulness, alcoholism, abuse—any number of influences that affect the way you feel about raising children. If you or your spouse have a history of such pain, it may be a good idea to seek godly counseling before you begin to have children of your own. You may need to address issues, express grief or loss, or forgive someone before you can move forward with a healthy family life of your own. If you are not the product of a happy family, rest in the assurance that you can be the first of future generations with a healthy, happy family life. God can do a new work in you. We are promised in Philippians 1:6 that "he who began a good work in you will carry it on to completion until the day of Christ Jesus."

Among our closest family friends are a young couple who have personal histories of unhappy family life. Their parents were divorced, and they married as new Christians and did not really understand what it meant to be a godly family. It has been a great encouragement to see how this husband and wife have begun a new way of life in their own family. They have committed themselves to spending time with older, more experienced Christian couples who are parenting role models. They are dedicated to praying for their marriage and their children. Their family is a lovely testament to how God can take a hurtful past and create a beautiful future.

5. *Who are your role models in parenting?* Certainly they are your own parents. This may be a good or bad thing depending on your upbringing. Each of us brings our own experience to child-raising, for that is what we know best. We all need models of godly parents. If you or your mate grew up in a home you do not want to emulate, it is crucial that you seek out other Christian families to spend time with. Observe how they operate. Ask questions about their parenting and discipline methods. Talk to other parents and to your mate about how you want to raise your children.

6. *Pray.* The Bible commands us to "pray continually" (1 Thess. 5:17). We should commit every aspect of our lives to prayer, for this is our lifeline of communication with our Creator. Should we not then ask God's direction in our family life? If it is our desire to walk in the path that God in his goodness has ordained for us, then we will seek his direction at every turn—especially in our decisions about when to have children. Pray that you would have a sense of peace, unity of heart as husband and wife, and clear direction from the Lord.

7. *Trust that God knows best.* Often our lives do not turn out as we anticipate. Perhaps you were surprised by an early pregnancy, or perhaps you are having difficulty conceiving. Perhaps the child you are carrying has been diagnosed with an incurable illness. If this is your story, God knows it already. He has gone before you in this plan, and it belongs to him. He will not lead you to a place where he is not present. He will walk with you through the trials, for he promised, "I will never leave you nor forsake you. Be strong and courageous" (Josh. 1:5–6). Do not hesitate to seek advice and encouragement from others who have walked the same path—you will need it. But know that, above all, God will keep

his promises to you and will give you the abundant life he has promised (John 10:10) in spite of any unexpected circumstances.

THE CHANGES OF PREGNANCY

When we realized that our first baby was on the way, we were thankful that God had designed pregnancy to last nine months! We knew we needed all the time we had to prepare for this exciting new phase called parenthood. What we did not realize was that, although we wouldn't meet our child for nine more months, we were already parents, and the changes were well under way.

Pregnancy itself was one of the aspects of parenting for which we were least prepared. Of course, we knew that nausea and strange food cravings were likely to affect me. We knew I would gain weight, that I wouldn't have a menstrual cycle again for a long time, and that I might be a little tired from all the changes in my body. We thought we were prepared. How mistaken we were.

We were both unprepared for the vast and immediate changes that took place. I felt as if the "me" I had once known had completely disappeared and a stranger had taken over my body, mind, and emotions. I did not understand what was happening to me—and my unsuspecting husband had even less of an idea. I became furiously angry, miserably depressed, giddily excited—all within a matter of minutes! I could not control my emotions at all, and neither of us realized quite what was happening—or that it was entirely normal. It took awhile to understand that these emotions were due to the vast hormonal changes taking place in my body. And once we understood this from a medical perspective, it didn't make things better! I continued to feel like a complete stranger to myself, and my husband thought he had permanently lost the wife he knew and loved.

It would take an entire book to describe the changes that pregnancy brings to a woman *and* to a man. Men do not become pregnant, but they do face many of the symptoms of pregnancy their wives do—especially the emotional changes. We highly recommend that you and your spouse discuss with your obstetrician, as well as with close friends who have had children, the changes you can expect during pregnancy. It is encouraging to understand what is happening and why, and it is reassuring to know that others have experienced the same highs and lows as you. Let us discuss a few of the most obvious changes that take place.

Physical changes to the woman's body are the most immediately noticeable. Long before her abdomen begins to show growth, other changes have taken place. She will feel continuously exhausted. Her breasts will grow larger and will be very tender and sore for the first couple of months. A woman's skin also changes—from being increasingly dry to having overproductive oil glands. Her waist will thicken, and she will begin to feel "just plain overweight" weeks before it is obvious to anyone that she is with child. Many women are delighted by the changes in their body—others are not. This is a time when husbands must be particularly sensitive to their wives' feelings.

Along with the physical transformation comes even more mystifying emotional changes. Many of these are linked to hormones; others simply are a woman's reaction to the physical changes in her body. A wife may feel quite uncomfortable with her bulging body and want to hide it from her husband. As mentioned earlier, she may experience a sense of loss of her own identity and a loss of control over what is happening to her. This can be confusing to both husband and wife.

The intimate relationship between husband and wife may become strained in many ways as well. Because a pregnant woman is often uncomfortable with her changing body, she may not want to make love with her husband. Often hormonal shifts decrease a woman's libido in pregnancy. In some cases, though, these same hormones cause an increase in sexual fervor. This may be a wonderful thing—or an awkward thing— as a husband's desire for his wife may change as he sees her body change. He may worry that sexual intimacy will hurt the baby or his wife (in all but the rarest cases it will not), and he may be unsure of how to express his physical desire in a way that is pleasing to his wife.

These are changes that every expectant couple will face. When you approach these things with honesty and a sense of humor, you will be able to make it through the awkwardness. It is important to have a sense of perspective and remember that everyone goes through these strange changes, and that there is a reason for them: The end result of this long process is a baby!

About halfway through the pregnancy the baby will make itself known in increasingly obvious ways. A woman will be able to feel fetal movement within her weeks before her husband can feel it on the outside. This will be very exciting for her but can be frustrating for him, as he will be impatient to feel his child's movements too. He may experience feelings of jealousy that his wife has such an intimate relationship with the child and he doesn't; and the wife may be frustrated that her husband "just doesn't understand" how she feels about the baby and the changes in her body. It is not uncommon for a sense of emotional distance to develop between mates as they wait for the child to arrive. This is why it is so important that the husband and wife have a sense of intimacy and unity *before* they become pregnant.

The first pregnancy is an opportunity to savor the time you have together as "just the two of you," for though you will have time alone together in the future, it will not be quite the same. Take time to talk about how you are feeling about the changes pregnancy causes. Husbands, be careful to express to your wife how much you love her and her changing figure! Wives, have patience with your man, as he truly cannot understand what is happening to you. It is the privilege of a woman to bear a child, a gift that should not be taken lightly by either gender.

Above all, have fun with each other. It is good to forget that you are pregnant every once in a while. Delight in each other. Remember who you are as individuals and mates. Do the things you did when you were dating. Have "dates" where you talk about anything except the baby. This time of anticipation is a gift to be enjoyed. Rejoice in the miracle that God is working before your very eyes. Pray together for your child. Read Psalm 139 often and remember that we are each fearfully and wonderfully made. This Scripture inspires awe at the miracle happening within you, and it can be especially meaningful if you pray it aloud, using the potential names you have chosen for your child. For example:

> For you created Caroline's inmost being;
>> you knit her together in Allison's womb.
> We praise you because she is fearfully and wonderfully made;
>> your works are wonderful,
>> we know that full well.

vv. 13–14 adapted from NIV

There are many questions to consider regarding the "big moment"— the arrival of the child. Taking a childbirth preparation course together is helpful. Your obstetrician will be able to recommend one to you. These courses cover many important issues regarding labor, delivery, and infant care. Will you have pain medication during delivery, or will you have a "natural" birth? Will the husband or any other family members be present during the delivery? Will you breast feed or formula feed your baby? There are no right or wrong answers to these questions. How you choose to answer them will depend on your personal preferences. The most important thing is that you address them and come to agreement about them before the big day arrives.

AFTER THE BABY ARRIVES

When your child arrives, you will feel as if a whole new world has been created just for you. You will be elated, proud, apprehensive, and grateful. But will you remember whose child this is that you hold in your arms?

This may seem like a strange question. "This is our very own child," you will think, "given to us by a gracious heavenly Father to love and to care for." This, however, is not the complete truth. Our Father gives us precious children to raise and nurture through life, but they do not belong to us, they belong to him. Couples may choose different ways to acknowledge that their children belong to God. Some believe that a public infant baptism or dedication is the most natural way to do this. This is not to make the child a Christian, but to demonstrate to the world that the child belongs to Christ, being a "child of the covenant." Our marriage is a covenant with God. Our children, therefore, are children of the covenant, and they belong to the Lord in a special way. We must recognize this and in a sense turn over the responsibility of raising our children to the Lord.

Not long after Jesus was born, Mary and Joseph did this very thing. The Gospel of Luke tells us, "When the time of their purification according to the Law of Moses had been completed, Joseph and Mary took him to Jerusalem to present him to the Lord . . . and to offer a sacrifice in keeping with what is said in the Law of the Lord" (Luke 2:22–24). They took their only Son, Jesus, whom they knew was born of God, and offered him back to the Lord. In this simple act of presenting their Son to God, they recognized that they were his parents on earth but that God was his heavenly Father. Jesus belonged to God, who gave him temporarily to Mary and Joseph for his life on earth. Though certainly Jesus came to serve a far greater purpose than any human child, the same principle applies. We must deliberately acknowledge that each of our children belongs to the Lord. In our family, we have a special time of prayer when each child is a week old, during which we present, or "give back," the child to the Lord and ask guidance in raising him or her.

Giving up our children to God's control in a way gives us freedom. We know that God loves and cares for our children perfectly, more than we in our weakness will ever be able to love them. He will fill in the gaps when our parenting is imperfect. When our children misbehave, we need not be devastated, because we know they belong to the Lord. When they excel, we do not take all the credit, because they belong to the Lord. We are simply stewards of our children for a short time.

As stewards of God's precious children, we are given an incredible privilege. What a challenging yet joyful task it is! One of the greatest surprises Will and I have discovered in parenting is just how much *fun* it is. Oddly enough, this is something we did not expect. One hears over and over the challenges and struggles of parenthood, but so often we forget to tell of the moments of hilarious laughter and wonder. We discover the world again as we watch our children experience it for the first time. And we learn surprising things about ourselves as we parent our children. Above all, we begin to grasp in new ways how great is the Father's love for us, as we feel our hearts expand with love for our own.

QUESTIONS FOR REFLECTION

1. What does it mean to you to be complete in Christ? As an individual? As a partner in marriage?
2. What was your family life like as a child? What habits do you want to repeat in your own family? What practices would you like to change? How will you discipline your children?
3. Discuss your ideas of the father's and mother's roles in parenting. How do these differ? In what ways will they complement one another? How will this apply to your family?
4. What does it mean to you to let God be in control of your family life? In what ways is this hard for you? In what ways does it come naturally?
5. If you do not yet have children, discuss your feelings about having them. How do you anticipate this changing your life?

He tends his flock like a shepherd:
He gathers the lambs in his arms
and carries them close to his heart;
he gently leads those that have young.

Isaiah 40:11

6

Motherhood
Susan

For me, motherhood arrived with a bang. Our oldest child, Allison, had just turned seven, and our boys, John and Chris, were four and two when we were surprised with twin girls. In a flash I joined the ranks of overwhelmed mothers.

When the twins were six weeks old, we moved from Pennsylvania to the Virginia–Washington, D.C., area. I had no family nearby, no friends, and no help. It was all I could do to stagger through the day praying that at least one child would fall asleep.

I soon discovered that many of my expectations of the kind of mother I would be weren't turning out as I thought they would. I remember noticing mothers out in public with their children. Many of their children were dirty. Green mucus ran from their noses into their mouths, their clothes didn't match, their hair was a mess. *When I have children they are at least going to be clean in public*, I promised myself. And then I had kids!

One day when the twins were eighteen months old I couldn't find them. Losing twins that age means one thing—trouble. Our son John was anxious because he had a soccer match he had to play in, and he was afraid he was going to be late. Frantically I searched the house calling out for the girls. Only silence answered back. Finally, I opened the door to their bedroom closet, and there they were—stark naked with an empty tube of greasy diaper rash ointment. They had squeezed out the entire contents of the tube and had covered each other's bodies with the sticky white goo. I knew we had to get to the soccer game on time, so I quickly put clothes on the girls and drove to the match, where I sat in the stands in complete humiliation as the twins ran up and down the sidelines with dirt and grass sticking to their ointment-covered bodies. How far I had fallen from my commitment to have clean kids in public!

Sundays have always been hectic in our home, especially when the kids were little. Since my husband, John, is a minister, he leaves very early, so the challenge of getting everyone dressed and to church on time was all mine. One particular spring day, with a great deal of satisfaction we arrived at church on time dressed in our best clothes.

I was feeling very proud of myself as we strolled up the walk until Allison, looking down at her little sisters, got a horrified expression on her face and exclaimed, "Mommy, the girls don't have *anything* on under their dresses!"

I had completely forgotten to put diapers or panties on the twins!

During those early years I quickly learned that motherhood has many surprises. Even today, with our children all in their twenties and me now a grandmother, I'm still learning the surprises of motherhood. We never "arrive." I've learned that motherhood is a demanding calling and that parenting is a team sport.

CELEBRATING THE ROLES OF MOTHERS AND FATHERS

A mother is bonded to her child from the moment of conception, and the cutting of the umbilical cord in no way severs the deep emotional and spiritual union between mother and child. The name given by Adam to his wife, Eve, means "living" or "mother of life," which gives the idea that a God-given responsibility is conferred on the woman to enable the child to have what is needed for a full and healthy life. A mother has a unique ability to nurse and nurture, to suckle and assure her baby that a man does not have. In most cases a mother has a different and more intense need to be close to her child than a man has. While a mother's love for her child may not be any greater than the father's love, the mother has been given by God a tender, alert sensitivity toward her child and a fiercely protective instinct that the father often does not completely understand. Mothers seem to realize the necessity of giving time and attention to their children, and they are willing to make great sacrifices simply to be with their children, caring for them and nurturing them. The Old Testament prophet referred to this when he exclaimed, "Can a mother forget the baby at her breast and have no compassion on the child she has borne?" (Isa. 49:15).

Fathers seem more naturally to gravitate toward providing *for* their children by working to provide food, shelter, and the other physical necessities of life. Some families are now so organized as to allow the father to be home more than used to be the custom, and surely this is a good thing. Fathers can be nurturers too, but there seems to be a God-created connection between carrying the child in the womb, nursing the infant, and then nurturing the child during the early years that belongs uniquely to the woman.

While a strict pattern of father-only and mother-only responsibilities is not found in Scripture and both parents are clearly able to nurture children and provide for material needs by earning an income, it is not easy for both parents to share equally in the responsibilities of earning an income and nurturing the children at home. If one has the primary bread-winning responsibility while the other has the primary child-care responsibility, the home will likely have a better sense of balance, and each parent may have a greater sense of satisfaction. It may be necessary for both parents to work fulltime outside the home, but the children will certainly be closer to their parents if that is not the case.

God ordained that Joseph, Jesus' earthly father, take the primary responsibility of earning a living by pursuing his trade in his hometown, while Mary, Jesus' mother, concentrated on the daily care and nurture of the children. Both parents, however, were very much sensitive to and involved in the concerns of Jesus and his siblings. That this pattern has been the normal one across the years and throughout most cultures surely is no accident. The mother's heart is bound up in her child, and this enables her to connect, sympathize with, and guide her child in a way that is frankly often amazing to a man. Still, it would be wrong to imply

73

that the woman should have the major responsibility for training, teaching, or guiding the children. Over and over again Scripture teaches us that both mother and father have the privilege and responsibility in this area. Proverbs 1:8 says, "Listen, my son, to your father's instruction and do not forsake your mother's teaching." Moses taught that both mother and father alike are to teach, instruct, and discipline the child.

Mothers and fathers parent as a team, each bearing equal responsibility toward their children. Yet the ways in which they carry out their responsibilities are often very different. All mothers can rejoice in what is a holy calling. Motherhood is challenging and demands the best of a woman. Perhaps the greatest lesson I've learned is how much I need God.

MAKING YOUR RELATIONSHIP WITH GOD A PRIORITY

The first child is generally the most challenging, because when the baby arrives, you immediately lose much of your personal freedom. In addition, you want to be a great mom yet you find it isn't as easy as you thought. For me, number two wasn't as big an adjustment. Number three was a lot trickier because I only have two hands. But four and five really humbled me. Each of us will react differently to motherhood depending on many things: our relationship with our own mother, our parents' marriage, our expectations, our husband's expectations, our personality, our child's personality, the number of children we have, and how close they are in age.

No matter what our background, we all quickly learn that we can't be the mother we want to be apart from God. Before I had children I was in the habit of spending time alone early in the morning with God, studying my Bible and praying in a *quiet time*. As the children came, it was harder to get up and harder to find thirty minutes of uninterrupted time by myself. And if I had the time, there were still many pressing things to get done before the kids woke up. Often I would go for days without that time alone with God, and I would become discouraged and even resentful of the tasks at hand. I quickly learned how much I needed time with God to read his Word, to share my hurts and confusion, to seek his guidance, and to learn his wisdom.

Making time alone with God the first priority of my day has made a big difference in my life. Several things have helped me make this habit a blessing: having a specific time, a specific place away from distractions, a modern translation of the Bible, a notebook, and a pen.

Scripture holds thousands of promises from God for believers. For example, "If any of you lacks wisdom, he should ask God, who gives generously to all without finding fault, and it will be given to him" (James 1:5). Many times when I have not known how to handle a problem with a child I prayed for God to give me his wisdom. "God, I don't know what to do about Libby's biting. Please show me."

Romans 8:28 is another example: "We know that in all things God works for the good of those who love him, who have been called according to his purpose." I have prayed: "Lord, we are so sad at the way Jake, a neighborhood boy, is treating our John. Please use this awful experience for good in his life and ours."

And Philippians 4:19 says, "My God will meet all your needs according to his glorious riches in Christ Jesus." "Lord," I prayed, "I really need encouragement. I'm so down on myself. Please send me some encouragement today."

As you discover God's promises, underline them in your Bible. Write down things you learn in your notebook. If Bible study is new for you, there are many guides on the market. Visit a Christian bookstore and seek their recommendation. Write out specific prayers. It will be an encouragement later to look back and to see how God has answered.

As moms we all go through challenges and blessings, times of crisis and times of calm. Often the best lessons are learned in the most difficult times. The first two years after the twins were born were particularly hard for me. I was exhausted and did not feel like I was being the mother or wife I wanted to be. And I didn't feel like I was doing anything significant for God. I became discouraged and sad. In my quiet times I began to pray for God to teach me something. "Why am I feeling so discouraged? What would you say to me in this situation, God?"

During this period I found the Psalms particularly encouraging. David, who wrote many of them, was honest about the difficulties of life yet remained confident in God's sovereignty and care. Soon God began to show me that I had a problem with pride. Up until this point in my life I had been fairly successful with everything. But now, overwhelmed with five children, I did not see success very often. My self-image plummeted. I felt like a failure. Yet my feelings of failure opened me up to the tender mercy of God. I needed to learn that he loved me not because I was successful, or led Bible studies, or was a good wife or good mother. I surely wasn't! I needed to learn to confess my prideful nature and to learn that God loved me simply because I belonged to him. My quiet times became my lifeline, because I knew in a fresh way how much I needed God.

Whatever the numbers and ages of our children or grandchildren, we need time alone with God. Both my mother, who is in her seventies, and my mother-in-law, who is in her nineties, spend time every day studying the Scriptures and praying. Even at their ages they feel the need to nurture an intimate relationship with their heavenly Father. Both continue to learn fresh things from God. Their prayers for John and me and for each of our children are the greatest gift they can give us.

FINDING SOME GIRLFRIENDS

When I was overwhelmed with babies I felt lonely. My husband didn't seem to understand my exhaustion and frustration. Even though he had a demanding new job, he had a set of goals for which he saw results. He had people who appreciated him and told him specifically why. He had a sense of accomplishment. But a mother of small children doesn't sense a lot of accomplishment or appreciation day in and day out. The house that was clean this morning is dirty by evening. Your four-year-old is not likely to say, "Mother, you are doing a good job of raising me!"

A mom in your same type of situation will be more able than your husband to give you understanding. Another mother is more likely to empathize with the frustration caused by a lack of accomplishment than is your husband. She appreciates the monotony that can come from the daily routine caring of infants. I once calculated that I had done twenty-two loads of wash and changed 144 diapers in one week. Just counting gave me a sense of satisfaction and my girlfriends something to laugh about!

Knowing several other mothers who can encourage you and pray for you is vital. You need the companionship of other moms in the same season of parenting—moms with whom you can swap children or go to the park. If you have young children, reach out to another mom in the same situation. Begin a neighborhood support group for young mothers, and study a Christian book on mothering together. Many moms longing for support and friendship have come to faith in Christ through the outreach of a mothers' group.[1]

We need friends whose children are close in age to ours, but we also need friends who are older than we are. They give us perspective. For years I have been in a prayer group with Tucker. She is ten years older than I, and her kids are all older. She encourages me because she teaches me what is ahead, and I learn by watching her. It is reassuring to have someone to ask, "How did you handle back talk? What did you do about curfews for your teenagers?"

For years my neighbor Edith provided a cup of tea and reassurance when I was having a bad day. In her eighties she was a mother and grandmother many times over.

I would run across our lawn to her house, knock on her door, and as she answered I'd burst into tears.

"Edith," I would say, "I am such an awful mother."

"No, you are not," she would respond. "It's just the season of life you are in. You are a good mother. This too will pass."

Because Edith was several seasons ahead of me, she was able to give me perspective.

Female role models encourage us and also mentor us. Especially if you come from a broken or dysfunctional home, having an older friend to guide you is a tremendous help. And we must also be willing to be that older friend in some young mother's life. Titus 2:4 calls older women to "train the younger women to love their husbands and children."

KEEPING MY HUSBAND FIRST

It is all too easy in this busy time of life to assume you will work on your marriage when things calm down. But things don't calm down. Life only gets more complicated. Responsibilities and options increase, not decrease. In our child-centered world we must be careful not to put our marriages on hold. Our children's demands and needs are obvious, and caring for them can be a full-time job. Yet if we want our children to have strong happy marriages someday, they need to see us working on ours. We have our children with us for approximately eighteen years, but God willing we have our spouses for much longer. If we invest all of our energy in our children, when they leave home we may find ourselves with a shallow relationship with our spouse.

If you are at home, comb your hair and put on a fresh outfit before your husband comes home. Maybe you would rather greet him wearing a shirt with the baby's spit on it and frazzled hair. After all, it's your badge showing your hard work! But resist the temptation and meet him at the door well groomed. Celebrate his coming home by throwing your arms around him and telling him how glad you are to see him. Such treatment will make him *want* to come. In addition you are training your daughter how to be an encouraging wife.

We have already mentioned the importance of having a date night each week. We began this in the first year of our marriage and have continued it for almost thirty years. We haven't had a date every week, because inevitably emergencies come up. But we have kept our dates approximately 60 percent of the time. If we had not had our dates written on the calendar, we would not have kept that many! Your time alone need not be an evening. It could be a luncheon or breakfast. The important thing is that it is regular and private.

Getting away overnight a few times a year is also helpful. When our kids were small we would swap kids with friends so that each couple could have time away alone. When we had five it was harder to find someone brave enough to trade with us!

As your children see you putting your mate first, they will be observing a radical biblical truth instead of hearing the world's advice to work on your marriage later.

RECOGNIZING THE HIGH AND HOLY CALL OF MOTHERHOOD

Motherhood is a high and holy calling. Psalm 127:3 says, "Sons are a heritage from the LORD, children a reward from him." As moms we are called to be nurturers. Paul uses the metaphor of a loving mother to describe his care of those under his ministry: "We were gentle among you, like a mother tenderly caring for her little children" (1 Thess. 2:7).

The prophet Isaiah described in pastoral terms the example God sets for us as our nurturer.

> He tends his flock like a shepherd:
>   He gathers the lambs in his arms
> and carries them close to his heart;
>   he gently leads those that have young.
>
> Isaiah 40:11

78

I find it so comforting to remember that as I am caring for my little "lambs," God is gently leading me. He is carrying me and my children close to his heart. There is no greater privilege than being a nurturer. But what does this mean practically speaking?

Our Children Need Our Attention

That children need our attention sounds obvious, yet it is not easy. Much debate has focused on the question: Do children need quality time or quantity time? Actually it is not an "either-or" issue. Children need both. Young children need little blocks of time with Mom—reading time, craft time, play time, hugging time. You can schedule these. Yet you cannot schedule deep talks with teenagers. You have to hang around in case they suddenly develop the urge to communicate. It usually comes at a most inconvenient time for you—when you're in the middle of something or late at night. You have to put your own agenda aside and simply listen. Part of nurturing is being available. It makes children feel valuable.

When you are having coffee with girlfriends, share ideas for special family times. One of our favorites is bowling in the kitchen. When our children were young, we simply took plastic bottles of kitchen cleaning products from the cupboard and lined them up as bowling pins. Then with three tennis balls we took turns bowling. Often we would go for a nature walk. Sometimes we would buy or check out from the library a book about birds, flowers, or whatever interested the children.

Develop Sharp Antennae

Proverbs 27:23 says, "Be sure you know the condition of your flocks, give careful attention to your herds." I have taken this passage as encouragement to study my children. I pray, "God, give me sharp antennae that can discern the needs of this child."

We need to ask questions such as, Where does he need building up? Where does she need discipline? One of the special gifts God gives mothers is a sensitivity to her child's heart.

As God reveals specific needs, I then pray, "God, show me how to meet this need." My child may have a need that someone else should meet or that I must simply take to God.

79

In studying our children, particularly as they grow older, we will be able to observe their uniqueness. Their weaknesses and strengths will become more evident, and as mothers we have an unusual ability to encourage them.

Perhaps you have an eleven-year-old daughter who is particularly sensitive and easily hurt by "mean" girls in her class. Tears come quickly for her. When a friend is in pain she is in pain. Her emotions can be exhausting, and comforting her is a challenge. But a blessing is in store.

Take your daughter aside and explain gifts and weaknesses. "Sweetheart, you are growing up so fast. Growing up can be painful, but I am proud of the way you are growing and am glad we can begin to talk about more adult things together. I want to share with you about gifts and weaknesses. When I look at you I notice a young lady to whom God has given the gift of sensitivity. You care so much for people, and you long for approval from them. You hurt when they hurt. You have the gift of compassion. Mother Teresa was a wonderful woman with this same gift. She was used by God in so many ways. I know that God is going to use you in some amazing ways. But you also need to know that every gift has a weakness. A weakness of the gift of sensitivity is that you will overreact to people's criticism. You will have a hard time letting go of another's pain. You will have to work at not overreacting. Recognizing your gifts and weaknesses will be helpful to you as you grow up."

Articulate your daughter's gifts, explain her weaknesses, point her to a hero (role model) with similar gifts, and give her a vision for her life. Take some time to learn about her hero. It may also be helpful to share some of your own gifts and weaknesses with her. Pray together for God to sharpen her gifts and yours and to help you handle your weaknesses.

Pray with and for Your Children

We cannot talk about nurturing without mentioning prayer. It is so important that we devote an entire chapter to it (see chapter 14). As mothers we have a special privilege of prayer. Because we are with our children the most, we are aware of needs as they arise. God longs for us to come to him not merely at bedtime or mealtime, but throughout the day. Our privilege is to introduce our children to the daily reality of a relationship with Christ.

From the time our children were very small, when we said prayers with them at night, we would occasionally pray for the boy or girl out there whom God might one day send to be their mate. One night Susy prayed, "Dear Lord, please bless the boy I'm going to marry, and help his parents to be raising him right!" I hoped there were future in-laws praying for me as I raised my children.

One day Chris came home from school in tears. He was still a tender young boy, and his older sweetheart had spurned him for an older boy. He was devastated. Wrapping my arms around him, I said, "Oh, son, I am so sorry. I know this hurts so badly." As I hugged him, I prayed, "Dear Jesus, you understand rejection. You know what it feels like to be hurt because you were hurt. Please put your arms around Chris and comfort him."

After we had prayed, I showed Chris Psalm 30:5: "Weeping may remain for a night, but rejoicing comes in the morning."

"Son, I said, you are so sad now. But this verse gives you hope that you won't always be this sad. You will have joy again."

Recently I had to speak to a group of people far away. I was tired and did not want to make the trip. I shared my frustration with Libby, and she prayed for me. When I returned she called to ask how it went. The trip had turned out to be an unusually special time. Her prayers had sustained and comforted me.

Yesterday Susy called from her university. "Mom," she said, "please pray for my talk with my classmate Mary. We are having dinner together tonight, and I have such a desire for her to know the Lord."

Together we prayed over the phone for their time, for God to prepare the way and give Susy boldness. Late last night she called again. "Mom, it was so exciting. We talked for three hours. She shared things with me she has never told anyone. She wants to give her life to Christ and meet with me each week to study the Bible. God had really prepared her heart."

As you walk through daily routines, take advantage of opportunities to pray with your children as needs arise. Share your prayer needs with them. As you do this you are not only nurturing your relationship with them but are encouraging their own intimate relationship with the Lord.

REMEMBER GOD CHOOSES OUR FAMILY

As a mother I have found it helpful to remind myself that God has chosen my family. He gives to each of us exactly the children we need through adoption or through birth, in the exact birth order, with their unique natures. He gives us these children not only for us to nurture but also so that they might be his tools in our lives to help us grow into the women he created us to be. This includes even that strong-willed child, that stillborn child, and that child with attention deficit disorder. Every child is a gift from God, and God will use each one in a special way to mold us as we let him. We nurture our children, but God uses those same children to nurture us in our relationship with him.

QUESTIONS FOR REFLECTION

1. How has your personal view of motherhood been shaped positively? Negatively?
2. What qualities of motherhood are most important to you in thinking about your own family?
3. Think of an older mother with whom you may want to spend time in order to gain wisdom and encouragement for your family life. Will you call her this week?

Do not fear, for I am with you;
  do not be dismayed, for I am your God.
I will strengthen you and help you;
  I will uphold you with my righteous right hand.

Isaiah 41:10

7

Fatherhood
John

One of the most respected American leaders who served in two different cabinet positions with a former United States president was being introduced on a late-night talk show, and the host hesitated over how to introduce him. It is customary to introduce someone who has been in government by referring to his most important title. When questioned about how he preferred to be introduced, the man said, "Well, if you want to introduce me by my highest title, introduce me as dad to my children."

There is no higher calling than to be a dad, yet we get precious little instruction on how to do it. Fatherhood can be both exciting and very painful, because most of us men feel so inadequate. I certainly didn't know much about being a dad when three years into our marriage our daughter Allison was born. Two years later our first son, John, came, and eventually we had five children in seven years. What I didn't know then was that fatherhood was my most important job.

Taking Stock

It might help at the outset of this chapter to think about how you would respond to the following:

On a scale of 1 to 10 how did my dad do as a father?
On that same scale, how am I doing as a father?
I wish my dad had told me . . . .
I wish I could tell my dad . . . .

Think for a moment or two about a few of the words that describe your dad. You might want to jot them in the margin. Whether absent or present, good or bad, affectionate or incommunicative, fathers exert remarkable influence on children's lives and may be the most powerful influence in the family. The father certainly is not more important than the mother; however, in this age in which the role of men in the home has been so much underappreciated, we need to underline that the man's responsibilities are crucial. Most men long for their father's approval, and the way they live their lives is, in some way or another, in response to how they feel their dad felt toward them. There is no way to overstate the influence of a father on his children.

Three Roles of a Father

Every father needs to learn to carry out three simple roles—*overseer, shepherd,* and *example.* In a sense, a father has the same sort of responsibility for his family that a scout had toward those traveling with him in frontier days. He has the responsibility to scout out the way ahead and do whatever needs to be done to be sure that his wife and children have what they need—material, emotional, intellectual, social, and spiritual.

God wants fathers to be close to their children. The Old Testament ends with this prophecy of what would happen when the kingdom of God came. "He will turn the hearts of the fathers to their children, and the hearts of the children to their fathers, or else I will come and strike the land with a curse" (Mal. 4:6).

One may wonder what that curse might look like and also wonder if the huge increase in violence, teen pregnancy, broken homes, and so on is not indeed an indicator of such a curse in our own day and if, perhaps, that curse has resulted partially from dads not being close to their children. In the United States about 40 percent of young people are being raised in homes without their fathers. Almost 75 percent of American children who are living in fatherless households will experience poverty before the age of eleven, compared to only 20 percent of those raised by two parents. Children living in homes where fathers are absent are far more likely to be expelled from or drop out of school, develop emotional or behavioral problems, fall victim to child abuse or neglect, or commit suicide. The males are also far more likely to become violent criminals. As a matter of fact, men who grow up without dads represent 70 percent of the prison population serving long-term sentences in the United States at this time. It is no understatement to say that fathers are important to the well-being of their children.[1]

The life, habits, and character of a father are the basis for the model he presents to his children. Let us now look more closely at a father's three roles.

Overseer

In describing qualities that make a man worthy of leadership in the church, Paul wrote, "He must manage his own family well and see that his children obey him with proper respect" (1 Tim. 3:4). A father can't manage very effectively from a distance; he needs to be intimately involved with his family. So the male tendency to organize our lives as though our work were the most important thing is a mistake. Men must take responsibility for how home life is going. If things are out of control—Dad, you're responsible.

Fathers often fool themselves about how much time they really do spend with their children. Some time ago *Scientific American* wanted to track the amount of time dads spent with their children playing and interacting. First, they asked a group of fathers to estimate the amount of time spent with their own little children each day, and they received an average reply of fifteen to twenty minutes. To verify these claims the investigators attached microphones to the shirts of the children to record actual parental speaking. The results were shocking. The average time spent by these middle-class fathers with their small children was thirty-seven seconds per day. Their direct interaction was limited to 2.7 encounters daily lasting ten to fifteen seconds each.[2]

Over the last several years young children have developed the habit of watching enormous amounts of television every week. During these formative years of life, children are extremely vulnerable. If they are receiving only a few minutes of their father's attention every day but are spending untold hours sitting before the television, it doesn't take a genius to discern how these kids are going to develop their personal values. One family life specialist found that the three things fathers say most in responding to their kids are "I'm too tired," "We don't have enough money," and "Keep quiet."

I nearly cheered out loud some time ago when I read, on the other hand, the comment of a clergyman on refusing the presidency of his denomination. He said, "We could have worked out the details of the job, but the issue is how close I can be to my children in the next few years. They are not a responsibility; they are a joy to me. At this age they start talking to you and share what they think, and I don't want to miss it."

How does a dad learn to oversee his home effectively? First, he must learn to be prayerfully dependent on God. The prelude to successful parental leadership is prayer, and for a dad it means not only prayer for his children, but also for his children's father. The beginning of success is acknowledging your need for God. Ask God for his help and pray about the kind of dad you want to be—patient, available, wise, understanding. A wise father prays for himself.

Many times my prayers have grown out of despairing moments as a father. I have prayed, "Oh, God, this is too big for me." We need to pray for God to give us the knowledge, understanding, and wisdom we need to father our children effectively.

Leading at home also means being familiar with our children. For many years I've kept horses at our little farmhouse. Whenever I go there, one of my first tasks is to find the horses and look them over very carefully, running my hand over their head, neck, withers, and legs. I do this because I want to assure myself that everything is fine with them. Just as a wise person takes time to know his livestock, to be familiar with their condition, so we apply this principle to our children and are wise to ask ourselves how well we know them. They are changing all the time. Do you know the answers to questions such as the following? Who are your children's closest friends? Who are their teachers? What is their favorite music? What have they been reading lately?

Every year my wife and I set aside a special time to consider together each of our children, to talk about their needs and our concerns for them. We try to identify needs in each child's life in five areas: physical, intellectual, social, spiritual, and emotional. We list those needs as they come to mind and then discuss them. As the children have gotten older, it has become a family tradition to gather for an evening, having already prepared our own personal lists of needs and goals for the upcoming year. We share these personal concerns and pray for one another.

My wife has a much more informed set of observations about the children than I do. One year, however, I was able to take several months off work, and we were able to spend time together as a family traveling, vacationing, and living in different communities. During this time I was never separated from the children. At the end of that time, when my wife and I sat down to discuss the children's needs, I was every bit as knowledgeable of their condition as she was. This underlines a simple truth that the more time you spend with your children, the more you understand their needs. Listen to your children's mother when she talks about her observations of the children, because she will often have more insight than you do. Intercede for your children each day, praying through their schedules, burdens, decisions, and responsibilities, and talk to them about these things daily.

My wife developed something we call "the clue-in principle" several years ago. Often, before I would leave work to come home, she would call me to "clue me in" about something I should be aware of concerning one of the children when I came home that night.

"We have a growling teenager tonight—child number three. Got it?"

"Right, I've got it, and I'll be right home."

The wise father seeks to understand his children's world. Walk through their day with them sometime—ride the school bus or visit their school and walk down the hallways, hang around at athletic practice after school, talk to their teachers. Do this to recall what it feels like to be a child in school again. Some of my greatest memories center on trips I've taken to visit my children over the last few years—staying with them at their college, visiting the city where they are working, taking trips with them. One of our sons has been living in London for several years, and we have made a point to try to be with him in his London flat, getting to know his friends and seeking to understand his world. The other son spent a significant amount of time on a ranch in Wyoming, and both my wife and I made time to go out and be with him so that we could better grasp the significance of this experience in his life. Talk to your children's teachers, perhaps the youth pastor of your church if you have one, and others who are around your children, and ask them to explain what your kids are going through emotionally, physically, and so on. Discuss what you learn with your wife with the aim of understanding your children. Every father needs wisdom, and none of us starts out wise—wisdom must be learned. We learn from experience and from other dads, so talk to other men and learn from their experiences with their children.

Shepherd

The apostle Peter, writing to church leaders, gave the following guidance: "Be shepherds of God's flock that is under your care, serving as overseers—not because you must, but because you are willing, as God wants you to be . . . being examples to the flock" (1 Peter 5:2–3). If we don't shepherd our children, who will? They always need it, no matter how old they are. We do this by being sensitive to their needs in the same way a shepherd is sensitive to the needs of his sheep and gently cares for them.

What situations are your children facing now? What will they face in the future? Think through these questions. Anticipate issues such as coping with peer pressure; encountering strangers; being tempted to use alcohol, drugs, or tobacco; joining an athletic team; controlling sexual feelings; making good grades; preparing for college; getting a job; and choosing a marriage partner. The wise shepherd sees these situations as great opportunities to minister to his children.

Some men almost seem to resent their children at times and miss out on some of life's greatest joys, which come from making sacrifices to care for them. Many years ago Bill Havens, an Olympic rowing favorite, passed up the opportunity to participate in the Olympic Games in order to be with his wife during the birth of his son Frank. Twenty-eight years later Frank won a gold medal in the Helsinki Olympics and sent a telegram to his dad that ended, "I'm coming home with the gold medal that you should have won." I expect that Bill considered the sacrifice he had made years earlier well worth it when he received that telegram.

If you spend time with your children, they will know that you care for them and love them. I've observed over the years that it is often hard to leave something undone just to be with my children, but having done it, I'm always glad I did. In order to minister to his children, a father must do things with them—ride bikes, play catch, help them with their homework, and so on. Young children need our involvement in their lives in small segments of time, but as they get older they need larger blocks of our time. One of the ways in which my father influenced me as a boy was by taking me with him when he would go out to our family farm on Wednesday afternoons. We didn't talk together a great deal, but we were together, and not only did I learn by observing him, but my sense of security in his care for me was continually deepened because of his desire for me to be with him.

One day Charles Adams, the son of John Quincy Adams, an early U.S. president, entered these words in his diary: "Went fishing with my son—a day wasted."

His son, Brooks Adams, also kept a diary, which is still in existence, and on that same day he wrote, "Went fishing with my father—the most wonderful day in my life."

Brooks' entry gives assurance that you don't waste time by spending it on your children. Time flies by quickly; we can't save it or add to it, but we can invest it by putting it into our children and grandchildren. Fathers should never underestimate the priceless return they receive—both in this life and in the life to come—on the time they invest in their children. At the end of our lives we will look back and see that either we sacrificed our time for our children or we sacrificed our children for our time. This comment by a Harvard Medical School psychologist makes sense: "Children need vast amounts of parental time and attention. It's an illusion to think that they need to be on your timetable, and that you can say, 'OK, we've got half an hour. Let's get on with it.'"

Our children depend on us. They need us to be sure their needs are being met, and they often need to hear us tell them that we love them. Sometimes it's difficult for a dad to speak openly, tenderly of his love for his children, but they need this more than anything else. I've tried over the years in every phone call or letter of correspondence to close by telling my children that I love them.

When our children became older and began leaving home for extended periods of time, I always tried to express words to the effect,

"Honey, nothing you could ever do could cause me to stop loving you. I will drop everything and come to you anytime you need me."

Express your love to your children. Make notes in advance if you need to. I have often done this, because sometimes I don't really know what I want to say when the time arrives. It is worth whatever it takes.

Many years ago a song called "Cat's in the Cradle" was popular. From the very first time I heard it, it struck a chord of fear in my heart and warned me just how important it is to be the shepherd that my children need me to be. That song tells the story of a little boy who wants to grow up to be like his father, but the father is always too busy for his son. When the son is grown and the father retired, the father wants to travel to visit his son. He finds that his son has indeed grown up to be like him—he's too busy for the father's visit.

Example

A few years after my own father died I was meditating on the most important principles and truths he had taught me. I listed about twenty different points and then, upon further reflection, realized that I could remember my dad actually talking to me about only four or five of the twenty items. He taught me more by modeling these things than by his words, although his words have always been very important to me.

One of the most vivid images I have of my dad is that of seeing him on his knees by his bed in prayer every night. Who we are is what our children remember about us. Therefore, a wise dad realizes how important it is for him to be honest about himself with his children. He can, in fact, be honest about his failures as well as his achievements. Sometimes a dad needs to share with his children about some of his own inner struggles.

I recall vividly a day when I was fourteen when my dad shared with me about an extremely difficult decision he had to make. On that day I saw him in a new light: He was a human being just like me. Talking to children about tough decisions helps them begin to appreciate what it's like to be an adult.

A wise man periodically turns to his own soul and asks some hard questions about himself. Am I really the man I seek to portray to others? Am I a man of honesty and integrity? Our true character is found in who we are when no one else is watching. But our children are always watching.

A dear friend of mine struggled with a dark and secret problem for thirty-five years, and it was only through an accident that I became aware of this and was able to talk to him about it. He had very much wanted to discuss it, but because of his own deep shame, he found it simply impossible to reveal, even to me, his closest friend. After we had the conversation, it became easier for him to face the fact that he needed to take certain steps to overcome this problem. In time he found the courage to talk to his oldest son about it, because he knew this boy might be vulnerable himself, just as he had been. His honesty, humility, and concern for his son impacted the boy greatly.

A Christian man is shaped by his relationship with God, and only the two of them know just how genuine it is. God knows us even better than we know ourselves. A wise man will ask God to reveal to him those areas in which he needs to grow and mature as well as those sins of which he needs to repent. The strength of a tree is determined by the roots in the ground, and the strength of a man is always below the surface, out of sight. It lies in the depth of our relationship with our Creator. We must be honest about where we need to grow, face up to it, and ask God's help.

It is not enough for a man just to have his own relationship with God. A Christian father has the responsibility to pass down the truths of God to his children and grandchildren to the best of his ability. This means particularly that we have the responsibility to share the teachings of the Bible with our children. Some men make the mistake of thinking that it's a mother's responsibility to read Bible stories and discuss them with the children. It's the father's responsibility as well. If the Bible is important to Dad, it will be honored by the whole family.

We take to heart these words from the psalmist:

> [God] commanded our forefathers
>   to teach their children,
> so the next generation would know them,
>   even the children yet to be born,
>   and they in turn would tell their children.
> Then they would put their trust in God
>   and would not forget his deeds
>   but would keep his commands.

Psalm 78:5–7

I urge you to make a priority of reading the Scriptures and of getting a simple Bible storybook to share the Word of God with your children. You may not have been trained in the Scriptures as a child, and you can't teach what you don't know. But I am absolutely certain that the most important discipline in my life is that of taking a period of quiet time for Bible reading and prayer in the morning before the rest of the family awakes.

Similarly, a wise father will use whatever opportunities arise day in and day out to help his children understand how biblical principles apply to our daily lives. God gave this instruction: "These commandments that I give you today are to be upon your hearts. Impress them on your children. Talk about them when you sit at home and when you walk along the road, when you lie down and when you get up" (Deut. 6:6–7). In other words, we are to use daily opportunities to teach the practical implications of the Word of God. Some of the most precious conversations I've had with my children have been on the run as we have encountered certain situations that have given us the opportunity to talk about things that matter.

Pray with your children about a problem they're struggling with. Ask for their forgiveness when you need to. Explain to them why you have decided as you have. Tell them stories from your life. Share the principles you live by and why. In all these ways you can give them what they need.

You don't have to be a theologian. A wise father will simply see to it that his family reads the Bible, prays together, and talks about spiritual things regularly. You may not have done this up to now, but don't let that deter you from making the changes you need to make so that sharing the Bible with your children becomes a priority.

Derek Redmond, an Englishman, qualified for the 1988 Olympics in Seoul, Korea. Ninety seconds before his heat in Seoul he had to drop out because he pulled an Achilles tendon. Following that injury he had surgery five times, and amazingly he was able to qualify for the 1992 Olympics.

About a hundred meters into the 400-meter semifinal, Redmond fell to the track with a torn right hamstring. There was no way he could run. But he said to himself, "I'm not willing to quit. I'm going to finish this race." He worked his way back up, and hopping and half crawling he began to proceed down the lane. Then something unforgettable happened. Way up in the stands a big burly man jumped up. Wearing a T-shirt, shorts, tennis shoes, and a hat that said, "Just do it," he ran down the steps, pushed aside the security guard, ran onto the track, and put his arm around the young man. Jim Redmond, the father of this young man, carried him to the finish line.

Back home in England, Derek Redmond's mother and pregnant sister were watching the race on television. The mother was in tears. His sister went into labor. The crowd back at the Olympics was going wild!

Here's the point: If an earthly father cares that much about his son who is absolutely determined to finish the race, no matter how much he hurts, then how much more will our Father in heaven rush to the side of his son who says, "I'm going to finish, and I don't care how much it hurts." This is exactly what God says to us in Isaiah 46: 3–4:

> Listen to me . . .
> you whom I have upheld since you were conceived,
>   and have carried since your birth.
> Even to your old age and gray hairs
>   I am he, I am he who will sustain you.
> I have made you and I will carry you.

Don't give up in your goal to be the best father you can possibly be. Choose to be strong, persevering, and faithful. Choose to be mature. Choose to walk in God's ways. He will help you. The almighty God wants you to finish strong.

QUESTIONS FOR REFLECTION

1. How has your personal view of fatherhood been shaped positively? Negatively?
2. What qualities of fatherhood are most important to you in thinking about your own family?
3. Think of an older father with whom you may want to spend time in order to gain wisdom and encouragement for your own family life.

I will instruct you and teach you in the way you should go;
I will counsel you and watch over you.

Psalm 32:8

8

The Atmosphere in a Christian Home

Susan

As newlyweds John and I always loved to go to my brother Tucker's home for dinner. With his wife, Ginny, and their five young children, it was not a quiet meal. Their two-year-old's messy attempts to get more food in his mouth than on the table caused us to roar with laughter. Throughout the meal the children participated in the conversation. There was a sense that whatever they said was important. Each member of the family was treated with honor. A genuine naturalness marked the family members' interaction with one another. *This is what I want my family to be like,* I thought as I soaked up the loving atmosphere. Love, acceptance, and joy permeated this household.

I had been to other homes where the dinner table resembled a cold war. The mother was unhappy, as if she were resigned to an unpleasant

95

task. An irritable dad sat silently while children complained. Rudeness was ignored, and sarcasm replaced laughter. Tired, battle-weary parents rarely smiled. Togetherness seemed like an endurance test. The atmosphere was sad.

Each of us wants a home that radiates encouragement, love, appreciation, humor, and forgiveness. We want a home in which there is a sense of belonging, of being believed in and accepted. As parents we have the responsibility to create such an atmosphere, and as mothers we have a particular role in crafting a loving atmosphere in the home. Fathers certainly contribute, but mothers are usually at home more. This is our privilege. It is not a burden. Just as we often take the initiative in planning the décor of our homes, we also have the opportunity to create the atmosphere.

Sometimes when I'm cooking I become so accustomed to the different odors that I do not realize the overall effect on the house of various dishes in the oven. The family can tell if I've been cooking fish when they come in the door.

"Hey, Mom, the house stinks," a child will call out. "We need to put the sweet-smelling pot on the stove."

My child is referring to a pot of spices I often keep simmering on my stove that produces a pleasing fragrance throughout the house.

Likewise, the emotional atmosphere in our homes can become unpleasant without our even realizing it. We can become so accustomed to harsh words that we are not even aware of their pervasive impact. From time to time we visit another home where the atmosphere is pleasant, and we realize we have neglected to work on the atmosphere of our own home. Sometimes we fail to realize that creating a loving atmosphere in the home takes work and does not just happen.

Paul refers to followers of Christ as manifesting a "fragrance" or "sweet aroma" through which God will manifest himself wherever we go (2 Cor. 2:14–16). This aroma of Christ is what we want for our homes, because it means sweet peace and joy. Paul gives us two different lists of ingredients for an atmosphere that reflects the presence of Christ.

The fruit of the Spirit is love, joy, peace, patience, kindness, goodness, faithfulness, gentleness and self-control.

Galatians 5:22–23

Love is patient, love is kind. It does not envy, it does not boast, it is not proud. It is not rude, it is not self-seeking, it is not easily angered, it keeps no record of wrongs. Love does not delight in evil but rejoices with the truth. It always protects, always trusts, always hopes, always perseveres.

Love never fails.

1 Corinthians 13:4–8

These verses give us a beautiful picture of the atmosphere we wish would characterize our homes. As we examine just a few of these ingredients, we should remember that only God's Spirit can enable us to create such an atmosphere in our homes.

AN ATMOSPHERE OF LOVE

To truly love others means always to seek and serve their highest welfare. The home can be quite a difficult place where this love is seldom seen in the events of day-to-day life. Little children grab toys from one another. Young people say cruel things to their siblings and friends and form exclusive little groups. Adults habitually gossip and speak harshly. Developing an atmosphere that radiates love requires audacity, faith, and effort.

This development begins with our own personal understanding and acceptance of God's unconditional love for us. Sometimes it is difficult to believe that God would still love us if he really knew us, because in each of our own lives there are things of which we are ashamed and of which we know God would not approve. Yet Christ says to those who follow him, "As the Father has loved me, so have I loved you" (John 15:9). And the apostle Paul wrote, "God demonstrates his own love for us in this: While we were yet sinners, Christ died for us" (Rom. 5:8).

Of course, God does know us totally, yet his love is so great that he sent his Son to live and die as one of us that we might be reconciled to him. Nothing we do or don't do can change his love for us. We cannot increase it or reduce it. As we learn to trust first in the security of knowing that God loves us, it will help us to allow this love to come into our homes. When the love of God begins to touch the atmosphere of our homes, this love produces three characteristics—sacrifice, acceptance, and appreciation.

Love Makes Sacrifices

Selfless service to others does not come naturally to us. We see this in our own homes. The husband might assume that it is his right to sit in front of the fire after a long day's work. His wife might expect him to help her move furniture or to help get the children into bed. The son doesn't want to do the dinner dishes, because it's not his job, and the daughter doesn't want to help with the baby, because she has other plans. Sacrificial service is not something we do naturally. But we must regain this principle in our homes if we want the atmosphere to be characterized by love. We cannot have love without sacrifice.

It helps to view our serving of one another as an offering to God. For example, mothers of small children are servants in caring for their needs. We do it because we are committed to and responsible for them, even though we get tired and often feel unappreciated. If we can view our service as an offering to God, the focus shifts away from ourselves and over to God, and we receive a sense of joy and satisfaction in the midst of our duties.

One of the ways we communicate love to our mates is by serving them. My husband tries to keep my automobile clean for me even though he despises the task. I try to keep the front steps of our house swept clean because I know it is important to him, even though I'm more concerned about the inside of the house.

Children must be taught the importance of service from a very young age, and family chores are an obvious place to begin. Even toddlers can learn to pick up their toys, and preschoolers can learn to make their beds. When children begin school they can fix their own lunches and put their own things away. Every child should have chores that he or she is responsible for doing on a regular basis.

In addition, we want to help our children learn to do things for others without being asked, and so over the years we have sought to teach the children to surprise one another from time to time by doing things for their siblings. When the boys were away at camp, the twins helped me clean their room to surprise them. The boys were pleased when they returned, and the girls felt pleased that they had helped. A surprise plate of homemade cookies made by big brothers and left for little sisters communicates love. Staying up late to help a little sister finish her homework and getting up extra early to make time to fix a younger sister's hair are ways of serving that teach sacrifice.

Serving is made easier when it is appreciated, and little ones especially need to be appreciated. As children grow they must learn, however, that serving will not always be appreciated or recognized. Encouraging your child to shovel the snow from a neighbor's walk teaches the value of serving without recognition. Putting away a sister's clothes without being asked is a way of serving in the family.

Children need to learn the lessons of financial sacrifice as well. Many parents begin giving their children a small allowance, or pocket money, when they are young. Children should be taught to tithe, to give back to the Lord 10 percent of what they receive, usually by giving to the church. Teach that tithing is not negotiable, so that the child learns from the early days that the tithe is just the beginning of our financial giving to God, and that often we will want to give beyond that 10 percent. As a family we have often tried to contribute additional monies to special needs beyond our local church, like helping out a poor family or sending kids from another family to a Christian camp. Doing this anonymously and having the children contribute some of their money allows them to share in the joy of giving without recognition.

One family in our neighborhood used to spend Saturday mornings together working in the church yard when their children were young. Hardly anyone knew they did this, but it was their way of serving the Lord together as a family. The family that develops sacrificial service will be a family where love is practiced.

Love Means Acceptance and Appreciation

All of us desire to be accepted. A wife wants her husband's acceptance of her viewpoint, and a husband wants his wife's acceptance for how he works. We also want our friends' and parents' acceptance. An atmosphere of acceptance in our homes is crucial, because homes that lack acceptance are homes controlled by tension, nervousness, and fear. Family members who feel they are not accepted are insecure and uneasy. By acceptance I mean a willingness to love the person "warts and all," a commitment to the other person even though he or she may be doing things that are completely unacceptable.

99

In the world a person's value is usually determined by his or her productivity or success. In contrast the Christian home should provide us with the security of acceptance—a place where we are seen as valuable and loved people simply because God made us and loves us.

A friend who was considering the Christian faith had two common questions. First, she did not feel that she was good enough for God to accept her, and second, she felt that if she ever did commit her life to Christ, she would not be able to maintain her commitment. I tried to explain to her that none of us will ever be good enough for God and that our goodness has nothing to do with his love for us. We cannot wait until we straighten out our lives or begin to live up to what we assume are God's expectations of us. We must understand that he accepts us completely, not because we deserve it, but because he made us and he loves us. This is unconditional love. Of course we will fail him time and time again, and for this he has provided forgiveness. God certainly does not approve of all of our behavior, and neither will we, as parents, always be happy with our children's behavior, yet we do love, accept, and approve of them as people.

As we grow in our sense of confidence in God's acceptance of us, we find it easier to create an atmosphere of love and support in our homes. One way we do this is by showing verbal appreciation and recognition of one another's good qualities. Husbands and wives need to express appreciation and gratitude for one another in front of their children.

I remember my father putting his arms around my mother and exclaiming, "You are the best wife I've ever had." Of course, he only had one, and as a child I thought it was silly, but it made me feel good when Dad built up my mother. And consequently each of the children valued her deeply.

Recognize your children for the unique qualities God has given them. Applaud them and let them know you recognize what those qualities are. One of my daughters has an extraordinary gift of leadership. When she was younger, this gift sometimes got her into trouble, as it came across as bossiness. Yet as she has matured and learned more about using this gift, it has been a blessing to many. Once, after an unpleasant situation for which she had to be disciplined for giving everyone in the family orders, I talked with her about how special she was and how proud I was of the unusual gift of leadership God had given her. I promised her that we would work together on learning how to use this gift for good, and that God would help her. He has.

Showing delight in our children and in their activities by supporting and encouraging them is another way of commending them. Going out of your way to be at a soccer match or piano recital creates a sense of family pride and an atmosphere of love. Going to one another's events indicates that your family loves and supports one another. It's not unusual for the younger children to go to the performances or ball games of the older ones. But we should encourage the older children to be present at some of the younger siblings' activities as well. This visible expression of pride on the part of an older sister or brother goes a long way toward building family unity and acceptance.

When our children were younger we played our own version of Spin the Bottle. Family members gathered in a circle, and one person would spin a bottle in the center of the circle. When it stopped, the one spinning the bottle would tell the person to whom the bottle pointed something he loved about that person. That person would then take the next turn spinning. Once Libby, who was about three years old at the time, spun the bottle. When it landed on her big sister, Allison, she said, "I appreciate Allie because sometimes she lets me get in bed with her, and she doesn't get too mad if I wet it." This simple game is a wonderful vehicle for building up one another's sense of self-worth.

Wise parents do not allow negative attacks between family members. Children will naturally blurt out things like "I hate you" or "You're stupid," but we must create the expectation that they will treat each other with respect. If our homes are going to be places where we receive approval so that later on we can move with self-confidence into a difficult world, put-downs must be eliminated from the beginning.

I will always be grateful that my father used to say to me over and over again, "Susan, I am so proud of you."

"Why?" I would ask.

"Simply because you're mine," he would say.

Knowing that our parents love us this way helps us to understand God's acceptance and love for us as well. When children understand that family members are totally accepted simply because they are family, they gain a sense of peace and security.

Persons who are unappreciated tend to have a low self-image. Often we slide into a pattern of expecting others simply to do their jobs and maintain their responsibilities, such as cleaning the house, taking out the trash, preparing meals, or mowing the lawn, and we fail to appreciate them, because they are doing simply what is expected of them. Even when someone is doing a regular task that he or she is expected to do, we should show we appreciate it. Having certain standards of behavior and then appreciating the results is not working at cross purposes. I've expected my husband and my sons routinely to take out the trash without complaining, yet it also encourages them when I remember to thank them for doing it. We expect our children to speak politely, yet complimenting them on their good manners reinforces their behavior. We should expect high standards and then show appreciation when family members work hard to meet them. All of us need to be appreciated for the regular or extraordinary things we do.

We see such appreciation exemplified in the Scriptures. Paul understood the importance of appreciation. When he wrote to his fellow believers he continually expressed thanks for them and for their faith and encouragement. For example, he told the believers in Thessalonica, "We always thank God for all of you, mentioning you in our prayers" (1 Thess. 1:2). And, "We ought always to thank God for you, brothers, and rightly so, because your faith is growing more and more, and the love every one of you has for each other is increasing" (2 Thess. 1:3).

Frequently in his letters, Paul offered thanksgiving to God for different qualities in the lives of his friends, and he told them how he appreciated the different things they did. He teaches us the value of first appreciating God for what he has done for us. As we develop the habit of thanking God in our own prayer life, a joyfulness of spirit will overflow into our homes, and we will express gratitude to our family members.

The wonder of God's creation is a ready, constant reason for us to express gratitude. "Look at the snow, children. See how it sparkles like glitter? Isn't God good to make it so white?" "Look at the colors of these leaves. . . ." "Feel the warmth of this sand. . . ." "How great God is to make so many things look and feel so different. Let's thank God. Wouldn't it be sad if everything were the same? God is good. We're thankful to him." Appreciating with our small children the things that God has made will restore within us a sense of God's power that we too often take for granted.

When Allison was a toddler we spent vacations on my husband's family farm. Overlooking a grassy field was a large hammock tied between two ancient sycamore trees. Curled up together in this hammock swing-ing back and forth Allison and I made up a song together: "Thank you, Lord, for . . ." was how it went. We would take turns filling in the blank. This became our special place of thanksgiving, and whenever I see a hammock to this day it reminds me of those precious moments. Thank-ing God in our own prayer lives and creatively helping our children to be thankful to God will open the way for appreciation to become more natural in the home.

We constantly need to be expressing genuine appreciation to our mates in front of our children. For example, a dad might say, "I appreci-ate your carpooling the kids all over town today." And a mom might say, "I appreciate your working so hard to provide for us even when you would have rather stayed in bed today."

Sometimes in family prayer times it is good to thank God for some-thing special a family member has done. We will often go around in a circle so that each person can express gratitude to God for something that another person has done.

Write notes on napkins and hide them in your children's lunch boxes to tell them how thankful you are for specific things they have done. Children love such expressions of appreciation. Leaving notes periodi-cally to family members, praising or appreciating them, uplifts them and helps guard against taking one another for granted.

Training children to use good manners is another way of encourag-ing appreciation as well as teaching them about respect. Writing thank-you notes, for example, is a vital task for everyone. As soon as our chil-dren are able to write, they should learn to send their own little thank-yous to special people. We teach our children to say thank you to the bus driver, the hostess, and even to their siblings and parents, for this is crucial in learning the value of appreciation.

AN ATMOSPHERE OF FORGIVENESS

Another ingredient that reflects the presence of Christ in our homes is forgiveness.

One of our friends recently told us that over the last several weeks he had been extremely busy with travel and work that kept him from being home as much as he needed to be. He was tired and feeling guilty about neglecting his family. This caused him to overreact with the children, disciplining them unusually severely when he finally did get to spend some time at home. He was also impatient with his wife. Finally realizing what he had been doing, he called the family together and told them of his realization of his impatience and curtness. He asked them to forgive him for being away from them so much and for overreacting. This honest expression of how wrong he had been caused the children, as well as his wife, to express their love and understanding and deepened the sense of family unity at a time when they could have been further alienated from one another. Confession, apology, and forgiveness are important elements in a loving home.

Forgiveness enables tension to be released and peace to return to our homes. Unless forgiveness flows freely, bitterness and resentment can seep in. Practicing forgiveness is difficult unless we have first accepted God's readily available and abundant forgiveness. Grateful for Christ's death on the cross as payment for our sins, we humbly go to God, confidently asking him to forgive us. As we experience this in our own lives, we are enabled to forgive others. Forgiveness runs deeply through nearly every page of Scripture. How can forgiveness similarly permeate the atmosphere of our homes?

Our first responsibility is for our own relationship with God, so we must seek his forgiveness every day for our wrongs. Mothers surrounded by little children often will suffer bad attitudes that need to be confessed and forgiven in order for the atmosphere in the home to be happy and uplifting. For example, I may resent having to be closed up alone with small children in the house for yet another day, or I may be irritated toward someone I feel has not paid enough attention to me. Or I may be jealous toward someone who seems to have everything I lack. When I do not deal with such attitudes, confessing them as sin and asking God to deliver me from them and give me forgiveness, I become a critical, bitter woman and create an atmosphere of negativism.

As we begin to experience personal forgiveness, we are then more easily able to forgive others. We often do not *feel* like forgiving our mate or our children, but forgiveness has nothing to do with feelings. We forgive because God has told us to forgive, and forgiveness must occur before healing can take place. When forgiveness is offered, healing begins and feelings slowly begin to change, but this often takes a long time.

Recently I lashed out at Libby in an unfair manner. I was tired. It was the end of a long week, and I held her responsible for something that was not her fault. I knew I needed to ask her to forgive me, but I did not feel like it. After all, I am the mom! But I have learned to go and get things straight. Knocking on her door, I said, "Libby, I'm so sorry I treated you unfairly, and I need to ask you to forgive me. Will you forgive me?"

In her tears she managed to say yes, and I prayed with her, asking God to forgive me for mistreating her and thanking him for his forgiveness. This restored our relationship, and we were able to begin anew.

In the Christian home we dare not allow wrong relationships to continue without dealing with them, and we dare not leave apologies unsaid. We must be committed to right relationships, because when relationships are wrong the atmosphere in a home becomes clouded and dark.

Perhaps forgiveness was missing from your home when you were a child. Perhaps abuse or alcoholism or divorce occurred. You must not let this past control you, and the key to this is forgiveness. We must learn to forgive our parents and look to God for his help in healing us. If we are unable to work through this on our own, it is important to share our situation with a few close friends for their encouragement and prayer or to meet with a wise counselor.

An Atmosphere of Joy

When love and forgiveness are missing from the atmosphere of a home, a lack of joy results. Even the godliest families are not always happy. Frequently the normal chaos of life produces tears. Sometimes it seems we can only endure what goes on. But God has a deep joy he desires for us to experience—joy in his presence, in our situations, and in our families.

This joy is supernatural and refreshing. Supernatural joy grows out of our relationship with the Lord. It is the second "fruit of the Spirit" (Gal. 5:22) and is distinct from happiness. Happiness is usually caused by circumstances. We feel happy when things are going well but feel down or depressed when life is not going well. Supernatural joy, however, grows out of a sense that we are resting in God's loving arms whatever our circumstances might be. When we remind ourselves of our security in him, we are free to relax and trust him whatever our momentary situation. We do not always feel happy, but we have a deep sense of joy that we belong to God and that his plans for us are good. Joy is his gift to us, and it refreshes us.

Too often we forget to be thankful, but praise and thanksgiving to God produce a spirit of joy within. I do not wake up easily in the mornings, and getting up is difficult. But I try to take a few minutes before I get out of bed to give thanks to God. When I do this I find that I enter the day with a positive attitude rather than a negative one. There are at least two types of praise: thanking God for who he is and praising him for what he has done. A simple prayer might go like this:

> Lord, thank you that you are powerful and that when my household seems chaotic you are still in charge. You know each of my children; you made them, and you alone are perfect love. You love my children even more than I do. Your goodness is overwhelming. Thank you, Lord.
>
> Thank you, dear Father, for the things you have done. You have given us this home and these children. They are healthy. You have given me a husband who loves his family, and you have provided all of our needs. Thank you, Lord.

Cultivating a habit of praise and thanks also makes it easier for us to praise one another in the family.

Some people seem to come into the world with a positive nature, always being able to look on the bright side of things, whereas others have a more negative outlook. In any given home you might have a mix of both kinds of persons. It can be quite difficult to live with a negative child or mate, but it is possible to cultivate a positive nature even in those for whom it is not natural. This is why it is so important that we regularly make time for family prayers of praise and thanksgiving. The evening meal might be an appropriate time for each person to thank God for something special he or she has done that day.

A person's outlook often reveals what that person thinks about. Paul admonished, "Finally, brothers, whatever is true, whatever is noble, whatever is right, whatever is pure, whatever is lovely, whatever is admirable—if anything is excellent or praiseworthy—think about such things" (Phil. 4:8). What our mind dwells on will determine in part whether we are a joyful or a complaining person. Developing the habit of discussing good things as a family helps everyone develop a more positive spirit. And so in family discussions, raise questions such as, "What was something good that happened to you today?" "What did you most enjoy at school today?" "What toys do you most enjoy playing with?" or "What book do you like the best?" As we talk about things and people whom we enjoy, we train ourselves in appreciating goodness rather than focusing on things to complain about. Wise parents pray for God to cultivate a positive spirit in each child and in themselves as well.

We have always wanted our home to be a place in which laughter was often heard ringing throughout. Laughter is one of God's great medicines, and in our home life we desperately need to laugh. We pray regularly for our children to develop a greater sense of humor, and we pray that God will give them mates who have a sense of humor as well.

Laughter can cover a multitude of mistakes. It can ease the pain of many difficulties and failures and can relax a tense moment, helping shift it from hurtfulness to restoration. When we learn to laugh at ourselves and our situations, our homes become joyful places. We all take ourselves much too seriously, and humor can bring perspective back into a situation. As we laugh at ourselves, we create a sense of lightheartedness in the family. This certainly does not mean, however, that we laugh at one another's pain or hurt. Sarcastic humor is seldom helpful and is usually destructive.

Nurture a sense of humor in the family. Purchase a joke book and keep it by the dinner table. Collect funny lists off the Internet to share. Learn to tell funny stories together. Turn mealtime into a celebration.

We moms especially need to develop the quality of being able to laugh at our situations. Sometimes playing practical jokes in the home or doing silly little skits can add a needed dimension of humor. We have to choose our practical jokes carefully, but when we play happy little jokes on one another, we can bring much fun into the home.

Sacrifice, acceptance, forgiveness, and joy are all crucially related to the loving atmosphere God desires to develop in our homes. Children who grow up in this atmosphere will be emotionally and spiritually healthy. They will be secure and will know how to build loving homes themselves. We have all the resources of God himself to draw upon, so we need not feel incapable. God will work with us to create this loving atmosphere. Indeed, this is his plan.

Questions for Reflection

1. Which statement or Scripture reference that you read struck you as especially important in shaping your family atmosphere?

2. Describe the difference between saying, "I'm sorry" and "Will you forgive me?" Is it difficult for you to ask for forgiveness? Why?
3. What are small steps you can take this week to help love, joy, and forgiveness grow in your home?

"Peace I leave with you; my peace I give you.
I do not give to you as the world gives."

John 14:27

9

Building Christian Character

John

Shortly after our twenty-eighth wedding anniversary my wife and I experienced both the sadness and the happiness of being at home alone. Our oldest child was married with a child of her own, our sons had both completed university and were pursuing their own adult lives, and our twins were well on their way toward completing their university years. With each of these children, the time came when we were forced to ask ourselves if we had raised them in such a way that when they left us and went out into the wider world on their own, their character would be mature enough to see them through the hard times as well as the good.

Some parents seem to think that their goal as parents is to make sure their children are always happy. Therefore, they tend to give their children whatever they want and say yes to most of their requests. They are, in fact, ensuring the eventual unhappiness of their children, for sooner or later everyone learns that life does not always bring us happiness. Life brings disappointments and painful challenges, temptations, and setbacks. Our job as Christian parents is to do all we can to ensure that our children have the endurance and stamina, the courage and dedication to carry on in the face of adversity and to be men and women of integrity no matter what. What is most important in life is not a child's education, athletic ability, good looks, material possessions, or accomplishments. None of these things is enough. Rather, a living relationship with God that produces Christian character is what will sustain a child, an adult, and a family.

Our goal is to raise confident children who have a sense of purpose and destiny in life. We work to raise young people who have a clear sense of who they are, what they believe, what they stand for, what they stand against, and where they are going. They must get this from their parents, and we cannot give it to them unless we have it ourselves. All our lives we too must be growing in Christian character.

Children do not just evolve naturally into godly people on their own. As parents we need to determine what character qualities are most important and work at communicating them to our children from the time they are very young. Our job is to equip our children for life, and training them in character development is the soul of this responsibility.

Some people believe that parents should let their children choose their own faith, values, and standards. This is absurd. For example, children do not naturally choose to be truthful; lying to protect oneself is human nature. Children must be taught the folly and shame of being untruthful. Truthfulness must be modeled, praised, and required in the Christian home. Parents have the responsibility to help their children make the wisest and best choices and to guide them into godliness. Children are like clay—they are pliable, and we must shape their moral character. Television, the media, and the cinema will not train our children to be charitable, patient, compassionate, and chaste. We must show our children the way and pray that they will indeed embrace godliness.

One mother understood this well. Her daughter had promised to complete a very simple but tedious chore early in the day before she would be allowed to get on with the plans she had set for the rest of the day. When the time came for the task to be completed and to take the little girl to her friend's house, it was obvious that the child had not fulfilled her responsibilities. The woman explained to her daughter that because she hadn't done what she said she would do, she couldn't play at her friend's house.

The child burst out crying and said, "But, Mom, don't you want me to be happy?"

This wise mother answered: "Of course I want you to be happy, because I love you more than you will ever know, but making sure that you always get to do what you want to do is not my goal. I'm trying to help you grow up to be a responsible young lady who is true to her word."

This mom knew her goals for her daughter. Children can manipulate us and make us feel guilty when we fail to do what they think we ought to do. But a wise parent remembers that he or she is building for the future, and always giving children their way is a shortsighted solution.

CHARACTER TYPES

A study of human character shows that there are at least four different character types. First, there's the person who does what works best to get what he wants instead of doing what is right. This is the self-centered person who pursues self-gratification above all else. A moral code is a secondary concern to him and important only to keep him out of trouble.

Another type of character is one who has no firmly established moral principles of her own but is instead influenced and shaped by those around her. She is the sort of person who makes decisions based on what she thinks she needs to do to please others. This approval determines moral decisions more than any internal sense of what is right or wrong.

The third type of person has a carefully worked out external set of rules and lives his life according to them. For this person the "why" of a certain behavior may not have been thoroughly grasped; what matters is behaving as one has been instructed. Your child may generally do the right thing but do it because he is expected to live that way rather than because he really understands why. Eventually he will ask, "Why bother?" and may toss aside his parents' values.

The truly mature person is one who lives a life in keeping with the moral values she has been taught and has come to believe in. She lives a good life not just because this is the way she has been taught, but because she has come to understand sound reasons underlying this type of behavior. Her moral behavior is not based simply on keeping the rules or maintaining family traditions. Instead, she makes decisions and takes actions based on her understanding of what is right and wrong, what is fair and true.

GOD'S PERSPECTIVE ON CHARACTER

Reflecting on the tremendous responsibility we as parents bear to help shape our children's character can be almost overwhelming. But we need to be joyfully reminded that true moral character isn't just a matter of family background, training, environment, or peer influence. Character is of the greatest concern to our Father in heaven as well. The God who gave us life and in whom we trust is the essence of pure goodness, and he wants his children to develop his character. Any person, regardless of his or her background or past, can grow into a fine and godly person. Jesus, the Son of God, always seemed to view people not from the perspective of who they were, but of what they could become. He taught the reality of new birth, of beginning again as a new creation.

God's Holy Spirit is even more concerned than we are about shaping our children's character, and he becomes our partner in the process. We must seek his guidance and learn to depend on him, trust him, and obey him. He will give us the wisdom to know how to help our children grow in goodness.

All of us are people in process, and it is God's intention that we parents be deepening our own moral character at the same time we are seeking to help our children become mature men and women. If we continue growing ourselves, we can help our children to do the same. If we are negligent in our responsibility, they will be as well. If we are impatient, unkind, and crass, they will be too. On the other hand, if we care deeply about others and make sacrifices to help others in need, our children will see this and follow in our footsteps. If we talk about how important it is to be patient and control our tongues, yet explode at the drop of a hat, our kids will be more impressed by our actions than by our words. On the other hand, if when we betray our own Christian values we admit it, asking God's forgiveness and the family's, that will make a huge impression on the children. Discuss often what matters most in being a person of godly character, and then live that way as your children's model. When you fail, honestly admit it.

THE VALUE OF CHRISTIAN CHARACTER

Our culture does not share our Christian understanding of character. The person on the street is not necessarily convinced that honesty, hard work, trustworthiness, courage, and all the other Christian virtues are important. Many people seem to believe that success in life is simply getting what you want, and if you have to tell some lies and break some laws in the process, it doesn't make any difference. Over recent years Western culture has witnessed unethical excesses in government and business that were undreamed of in earlier years. People are confused about morality. The most prestigious universities flounder when asked to develop courses to steer our future leaders through difficult moral issues. Ethics professors cannot agree as to whose ethics to embrace, and so we drift morally. As followers of Jesus, however, our model is Christ himself, and the virtues that he taught and lived are those to which we are called. We must have the highest expectations of ourselves and of our children.

At the heart of Christian character is integrity. Integrity is more than honesty; it involves trustworthiness, objectivity, fair-mindedness, sincerity, and thoroughness. A person who lives with integrity lives by the highest standard—the principles set forth in God's Word. He or she seeks to be the same in private as in public. A powerful illustration of this stands tall in the harbor at New York City. Years ago a popular American magazine showed a picture of the Statue of Liberty from above, and the amazing thing about the top of the head of the Lady of Liberty is that every inch of her hair and crown is worked out in perfect detail. It certainly must have occurred to the sculptor that once the statue was in place it was highly unlikely that anyone would ever see the top of her head. Yet it was still important to this artist to spend as much time on the hidden part of the work as on the face or the feet. This is integrity.

The home should be the first place where we live without pretense and where we are able to be real with one another. Is our home a place where we pretend or where we are genuinely ourselves? Parents set the tone. If we create an environment of openness that fosters honesty, approachability, and loving acceptance, pretense is discouraged and humility is encouraged.

Persons of integrity strive for consistency in their lives. They don't show one personality on Sunday and another on Monday, or one way of speaking with certain people and another with others. We should treat

113

all people the same. Children are often the first ones to point out our inconsistency. Once my wife was near the point of total exhaustion and was snappy with the children as she carried them in the car on yet one more errand. When they pulled into the gas station and she spoke to the attendant in a very pleasant voice, one of our children said, "Mommy, you weren't tired at him."

Our culture excuses a certain amount of dishonesty. But lying is unacceptable for the child of God. In our family lying has always resulted in strong punishment. Our children learned that it is far better to confess to doing wrong and to be disciplined than to lie. Children are surrounded by opportunities to cheat, whether it's in the sports they play, the quizzes they take at school, or family games. Watch your children at play. Correct them when they try to cheat. Tell them how important it is to be honest, and let them know that you'd certainly rather they did poorly on a quiz than copy someone else's work. We have always prayed that if our children cheated or lied, they would be caught, and this has happened on more than one occasion. Although unpleasant, being caught can become a great opportunity for growth and is a blessing.

There is much more to Christian character than just integrity. There is compassion, teachability, and courage. There is self-discipline and determination. This is not a book on character and is not the place to get into a detailed discourse on the subject.[1] The point, however, is that thoughtful parents will consider and often discuss what character traits they want their children to develop. They will realize that their children will develop these qualities only to the degree that they see them lived out in their parents' lives. Parents who are honest with their children about their failures but clear about the kind of lives they are trying to live will impress their children much more deeply than parents who pretend to be living a life they aren't. Be real with your children. Teach them the highest standards, and attempt with all your strength to live up to those standards yourself. Expect the same of your kids, but be gentle and understanding when they fall short. None of us achieves perfection in this life.

QUESTIONS FOR REFLECTION

1. How have your views on maturity of character changed over the years?

2. What qualities of mature personal character do you particularly desire to see developed in your children? Does your spouse share your commitment to help communicate these traits to your children?
3. Does "happiness" ever supplant other goals, such as duty, integrity, or faithfulness in your home? If so, how? Why? Is this a good thing?

The man of integrity walks securely.

Proverbs 10:9

10

Discipline
in the Home

John with Susan

I can still remember finding my wife exhausted on the back steps when I got home from work one day when we had three little children. She told me that she had spent the whole day in a difficult battle of the wills with our son John, who was two years old at the time. He is now a grown man and a son of whom any dad would be very proud. But on this particular day it seemed to us that he was likely going to grow up to be a terrible menace to society.

First, he had gotten into the cutlery drawers in the kitchen. He knew these drawers were off-limits because of their dangerous contents, yet he was allowed to play with the pots and plastic bowls in the cupboard. That morning, however, he had insisted on playing with knives and forks. After a firm warning he went right back to the drawer again. Then, after a spanking and an explanation, he shortly went back to the drawer again. It seemed as if he was saying, "I'm going to show you who's the boss here, Mom."

117

A second spanking didn't seem to help matters and incited a fit of anger, during which John pulled books off the shelf in the study and threw them on the floor. This battle of wills continued throughout the day with my wife trying to communicate to our little boy that, because she loved him so very much, she had to help him learn to obey. Eventually she sent him to his room, where his loud wails and sobs had caused her to be filled with doubt about her ability to raise these children and guilt about mistakes she was afraid she was making. John's older sister, who was four, did not help matters when she exclaimed, "Mommy, if you spank John any more, I'm going to cry!" We weren't quite sure who won the battle that particular day. The rebellious little boy went to bed that night extremely unhappy with his parents, but he did learn that disobedience would not be tolerated. In time he learned to obey his parents.

Nothing is more difficult in raising a family than discipline. If we're too strict, will we stifle our children's creativity? Are we expecting too much of them or not expecting enough? Are we somehow responsible for our children's stubbornness and willful rebellion? It is very easy to feel a great sense of failure in this area.

Western society has wrestled with the question of the best way to discipline children. I have a very vivid memory from my own childhood of being "switched" on the legs by my mother with a branch from a tree just outside our kitchen door. I never remember her spanking me in anger or not giving me an explanation, and I don't recall ever feeling that the parent who was doing the punishing did not love me. It was always clearly communicated to me that this was to teach me a lesson for my own welfare, and I believed it. I still do. But many parents do physical harm to their children in exerting corporal punishment, and none of us wants to fall into that trap. Physical abuse is a significant problem in more homes than most realize, and any punishment that even hints of cruelty is terribly wrong.

What is the right way to exert discipline with our children? Is there a right way? The Scriptures teach, as we shall soon see, that careful physical punishment certainly has an important place in child rearing. What is the role of the rod? When should it be used? When not?

Sometimes a careful, restrained physical spanking—whether slapping a child's hand, paddling his behind, or switching his legs—is appropriate. The pain must be sharp enough to get the child's attention but never harsh enough to do actual harm. A parent can easily abuse a child, doing him physical harm. This must never happen! For some children, simply raising one's voice is enough. Discipline must not be applied in anger. If a parent is not self-controlled, she should not touch her child roughly. Making the child stand in the corner or sit in a room alone may also work. Older children may be disciplined by removing privileges. The point is for the child to understand his behavior has been wrong and be made sincerely to regret it in order to avoid such behavior and consequences in the future.

There are two central purposes for disciplining our children. First, Christian parents want to raise children who desire to obey God. A child who has not learned to obey her earthly parents, whose voice she hears say, "I love you," and whose arms she feels in affection, will not likely learn to obey her heavenly Father, who she has been taught loves her even more. Second, we train our children to help them learn to manage their lives wisely on their own so that one day they can become completely responsible adults.

The writer of Hebrews says that God "disciplines us for our good, that we may share his holiness" (Heb. 12:10). So also, a parent must discipline his child, but as he does he should be asking himself, "How can I best help my child learn from this situation?" Suppose your child willfully disobeys a family rule. Simply punishing the child doesn't necessarily teach him the reason his actions were wrong. Ongoing discipline must be educational, or the child will profit very little.

God doesn't put love in opposition to discipline. In fact, discipline grows out of love. Without love discipline becomes hard and cruel. But love without discipline is just sentimentality. When a parent has maintained a strong loving relationship with her child, situations that demand discipline will actually bring the parent and child closer together.

When should we begin to correct and train our children? When they are old enough to understand the behavior we want them to practice. Two-year-olds can understand plenty! The first four to six years are crucial years for training children. These are the years when they learn to obey or to disobey. Waiting too long to expect obedience can be a mistake. Note what the Proverbs teach.

> My son, keep your father's commands
> and do not forsake your mother's teaching.

119

Bind them upon your heart forever;
  fasten them around your neck.
When you walk, they will guide you;
  when you sleep, they will watch over you;
  when you awake, they will speak to you.
For these commands are a lamp,
  this teaching is a light,
and the corrections of discipline
  are the way to life,
keeping you from the immoral woman,
  from the smooth tongue of the wayward wife.

6:20–24

He who spares the rod hates his son, but he who loves him is careful to discipline him.

13:24

Discipline your son, for in that there is hope;
  do not be a willing party to his death.

19:18

Folly is bound up in the heart of a child,
  but the rod of discipline will drive it far from him.

22:15

A word of warning: We don't want our children to think our love is tied to their obedience. A merit-based home in which parents withhold affection unless the kids are cooperative and courteous is no fun for the kids or the parents. Love and affection must abound at all times, just as our homes should be full of mercy, understanding, and grace.

Two very powerful factors influencing children are parental control and parental support. Control is the ability of a parent to manage a child's behavior. Support is the ability to make a child feel loved. Putting these two factors together is crucially important.

FOUR KINDS OF PARENTS

Parents generally fall in one of four categories when it comes to discipline, control, and support. Parents who are high in support but low in control are what we call "permissive." Parents who are low in support and low in control are "neglectful." Parents who are high in control but low in support are "authoritarian." And parents who are high in support and high in control are "caring."

What kinds of kids do these different types of parents produce? Caring parents (high support, high control) do the best job of raising children with a strong sense of self-respect. Similarly, when it comes to raising children who conform to the appropriate authority of others, caring parents do the best job. Interestingly, children who tend to accept their parents' faith are also the children of caring parents.

These things should not be surprising to us because of the biblical teaching "The Lord disciplines those he loves" (Heb. 12:6). He is the model for good parenting—high in support and high in control. Because of his love for us, he has laid down principles we need to follow if we're going to enjoy an abundant life. He brings about circumstances to discipline us when we fail to obey and instead turn away from the ways he has established.

If we want to raise children who will have the opportunity for a long and satisfying life, we need to give them the same thing—lots of support and strict control. Children whose parents lovingly establish limits and controls for them to obey have the greatest opportunity to find the fullness of life that God promises.

DISCIPLINE IN A CHRISTIAN HOME

The writer to the Hebrews said, "We have all had human fathers who disciplined us and we respected them for it" (Heb. 12:9). Evidently the writer had respect for his earthly father, because in being disciplined he learned that his father cared for him. If our children can see this, they will grow one day to appreciate the discipline we have given them just as this writer did. But they will not appreciate it at the time. We have to take the long-range view: What our children think of us now is not nearly as important as what they will think of us twenty years from now.

The means by which we discipline our children surely must change as they become older. When a child is young, sometimes restrained, physical spanking is the most effective way to communicate that an action is unacceptable. It needn't be harsh to get the point across. As time passes, however, other means of discipline become more appropriate.

Whatever method of discipline we use, it is crucially important to remember three things. First, we must let our children know what we expect—what is acceptable behavior. Second, we must be consistent. All too often the severity of punishment depends on the physical and emotional state of the parent. If you chasten your son on Tuesday for interrupting you on the telephone, when your daughter does the same thing on Friday, she should get comparable discipline. If a rule is worth having, it is worth enforcing. Third, we must always seek to reaffirm our love for the child in the midst of the discipline. Perhaps we should think of this whole process in the same way we think of training a child to ride horseback, ride a bike, or play soccer. We have plenty of patience in teaching a new skill because we accept and even expect mistakes. Perhaps we should see our children's misbehavior and discipline as a learning experience. When you see yourself as a coach or trainer, you will have greater patience.

Christians must live in obedience to God, and every Christian's will (self-centeredness) must be "broken" if we're going to submit to the lordship of Christ in our lives. We certainly don't want to "beat" our children into obedience to us any more than God wants our cowering resignation to his will. God wants us to rejoice in the wisdom of his commandments and gladly walk in his way. Likewise, we want our children to make responsible decisions and live a happy life in keeping with the Christian principles and virtues we teach them. Realistically, however, sometimes children don't see the wisdom of our teaching until they're older. In the meantime parents must enforce appropriate behavior with firm, loving discipline.

Below are some useful discipline strategies that will also aid children in developing self-discipline.

Present a United Front

Parents need to present a united front, agreeing on what is right and wrong, what behavior is acceptable and unacceptable.

If one parent demands that the bicycle be put away at night and the other doesn't think it matters, the child is going to be confused. Children need clear directions, not one opinion from one parent and a different one from the other. If one parent tends to be more permissive, the child is going to go to the permissive parent rather than the stricter parent, and this will obviously divide them. Mixed messages from parents will produce a mixed-up kid who will eventually become a messed-up adult. If we are going to handle discipline wisely, we have to anticipate areas in which our children are going to need decision-making guidance. Discuss these issues in advance and agree on what the expectations are so that you can present a united front to your child.

Observant parents will see in advance the issues that are coming. Are we going to make him go to Sunday school? Are we going to let her play on the soccer team at the same time she is taking piano lessons? What is our policy when he talks back to us rudely? What do we think about watching television, particularly on school nights? Parents must talk about and agree on these things even if it means doing research in order to come up with a united plan. Sometimes it is helpful to seek guidance from an older couple whose children are mature, disciplined adults. Also, many good books are available today that deal with questions of this sort.

Communicate Principles, Not Just Rules

I clearly remember that whenever I was punished as a child, my mother would explain why she was doing what she was doing. In this way she drove home principles of behavior for me to learn. She taught me that there are good reasons for punishment and that discipline grows out of love and concern. Jesus didn't just teach rules to keep, he gave us principles to live by, and wise parents will do the same. Rules are needed in households, but if our children are going to grow up knowing how to live the Christian life under constantly changing conditions, we have to instill in them unchanging principles in order to undergird Christian character.

When children are very small, we simply have to say this is right and that is wrong. But as they grow up, one of the greatest challenges is to communicate clear moral principles to them. A small child will not always be able to understand the why in discipline, and there are times when it is enough to say, "Because I said so." Sometimes as adults we are faced with obeying God simply because he says so. We may not understand why, but when as a tiny child we have learned to obey our parents, it will be easier to obey God as adults.

123

I particularly remember the difficulty we had teaching our sons to keep their bedroom neat. The room was almost always a mess, and I seemed to be constantly on them to pick up their things. One night one of them surprised me by asking, "Dad, why should we keep our room neat? It's our room, and we like it messy."

I thought about simply saying "Because I say so," but since they were teenagers, I realized they did need a few good reasons. "Well, son, first, this room is dirty enough now to be a certified health hazard. Second, if you don't straighten things up in here, you might trip in the night and hurt yourself. Third, nobody can find anything in this mess. I'll bet you can't even find your soccer shoes in here. Fourth, the rest of the family is offended by the chaos in here, and it smells bad! Finally, you both need to learn how to keep your life in order, and this is just one small step in that direction."

Be Strict When the Children Are Young, and Loosen Up As They Get Older

The first five or six years are the crucial years in which the building blocks of personal discipline are put in place. If a child won't learn obedience at home in the early years, the child's schoolteacher will have a very difficult problem. Little children need very clear instructions about what is acceptable and what is not. Once they understand, if they willfully disobey, they need to pay a price that will teach them to obey. The punishment certainly shouldn't be more serious than the disobedience deserves, but if children are repeatedly allowed to misbehave at a young age, they will continue to misbehave for the rest of their lives.

Often you will notice parents who can't seem to bear to discipline their young children. They ask their children to do certain things, and then when their children pay no attention to them, they try to distract them with something else. They suggest some other activity with the hope that it will change their behavior. But if that doesn't work, they either ignore the disobedience or overreact in anger. The children, not the parent, are in control in this situation.

When a child is young, parents must dictate her behavior, but as she grows older, it is more and more necessary for the child to decide for herself how she will behave. Many parents refuse to discipline a child when she is young, and then when a child becomes a teenager and his behavior is outlandish, the parent cracks down with discipline that is then no longer appropriate.

Give Your Child Responsibilities

Little children can learn to handle responsibilities a lot sooner than we might think. Giving your children jobs to do is one of the best ways to teach them self-respect, satisfaction, and responsible self-discipline. I remember thinking my wife was a little crazy when she gave our twins the responsibility of preparing their own lunches for nursery school when they were only four years old. But then I realized the kids seemed to get a kick out of it. Susan always carefully observed what they prepared, even though she let them do it themselves. As she explained to me, generally you shouldn't do for a child what a child can do for herself. It demeans the child and discourages a proper sense of self-responsibility. When children can tie their own shoes, choose their own outfits, and take care of pets, they feel better about themselves. Many parents tend to coddle and baby their children and then later wonder why the children are timid or afraid to go out on their own. When giving your children responsibility, be clear about what that responsibility is, and assure them of your confidence in their ability to do it. Provide help as needed. Always show appreciation and let them know how proud you are when they do a task well. Also, watch them closely to make sure they stay on top of their responsibilities.

Everyone in the home should have certain chores and responsibilities. For parents to do everything for their children is a grave mistake. Serving one another in the home is how we learn to serve others in life. Children need to learn to sweep the kitchen floor and help wash the dishes. They need to learn to pull weeds in the garden and rake leaves in the yard. Through such chores and duties character is built. Children learn to glory in a job well done and to do their tasks without complaining.

Appreciate the Value of Difficult Experiences

Many parents rescue their children when they are involved in difficult situations and thus rob them of learning a valuable lesson. Parents, forgetting that pain teaches vital lessons, are sometimes afraid for their children to experience any pain. Sticking with a sport, even when one is not very good and seldom allowed to play in competition, or sticking with piano lessons even when it's not fun and the child seems to be making little progress, is a very important discipline. Practice and work, day in and day out, teach us a great deal about life. We learn to push on even in boredom and pain rather than quit. We learn to rejoice in the success of others even when we are personally disappointed. We even learn to be content when we haven't accomplished all our goals, and that is a good lesson to learn.

Learning to wait is very difficult for children. They want success right now. They want everything sooner rather than later. We have to teach our children that we can't always have what we want when we want it. Delayed gratification is a valuable lesson to learn. If children learn to wait, they will be better equipped to wait when they are adults and things don't work out just as they had hoped. If we always let our children do what they want and have what they want, they will never learn perseverance.

Godly qualities are most often learned in difficult situations, disappointments, and times of pain rather than in happy times. Giving up on some endeavor may not be the best solution. You may unwittingly cause your children to develop a habit of quitting when the going gets tough. Help your children think through the commitments they make, and then consider carefully before you allow them to back out of a commitment once it has been made.

Be Honest with Your Children about Your Own Personal Struggles with Self-Discipline

Many kids tend to believe that their parents, since they are always correcting and disciplining them, must have no problems in their own life being obedient and disciplined. We will let our children down if we silently imply that when you become an adult you don't have a problem with this anymore. Children need to know that we never reach the point in life when, just like a machine, we always do what we need to do.

I vividly remember both my parents at different times explaining to me areas in their own lives in which they were having trouble exercising self-control. This helped me to realize they were human just like me. While our children know this, of course, they tend to forget it. Regularly we adults face temptations or difficult experiences we do not know how to handle. Sometimes we fail. Because children need to understand this aspect of being an adult, it is important to share some of your temptations and failures with them.

Perhaps you have a problem with procrastination. Talk to your child about this and ask her to pray with you that God would help you to be more disciplined. Ask her to encourage you. One dear friend had smoked cigarettes all her adult life. Then, in her older years, she had come back to the church and established a relationship with God and wanted to give up this bad habit. She was not making any progress toward that end until she shared her problem with the kids in her Sunday school class. They listened very attentively, and when she asked them to pray for her, they took it very seriously. She later found that, after the children began to pray for her, she was indeed able to stop her tobacco habit.

When we are willing to admit our weaknesses, we show our children that we are human and that however old we are we still live by grace. Every one of us must ultimately depend on the grace and mercy of God to get through life. If we can help our children understand this when they are young, they will have happier adult years. It will help them in their own marriages and with their own children. They will laugh, perhaps, as they remember how we chastised ourselves over our own failures. One of the most important memories a child can have is of his or her parent failing yet being honest and growing through it.

Distinguish between Honest Mistakes and Willful Disobedience

When a child knows he is being disobedient, he needs to be disciplined. When you tell your child to stay in his room and he goes out into the garden, that's disobedience. But when a child spills his milk at the table, that's a mistake. When a child is willfully disobedient, the consequences should be firm and swift, whereas the consequences of mistakes should be lenient and teaching oriented. Teach your child to keep his glass far enough away so that he doesn't knock it over.

It is also beneficial to help your child distinguish between critical and secondary issues. Some things are crucially important, but many issues are not so important. Truth telling is crucial, whereas, for instance, wearing clothes that match is secondary. A wise parent wants to avoid having too many rules, and so we need to be flexible on secondary issues.

FINAL THOUGHTS

Wise parents want to aim at a balance between saying yes and saying no to their children. Parents who are too strict create a stifling, negative atmosphere in the home and produce children who gradually begin to feel that nothing they can do will be good enough to please their parents. But parents who are too lenient will see their children grow up and become self-centered, rude, and obnoxious. We want balanced homes in which the word *yes* is used over and over again and children understand clearly what behavior is expected. Parents can be in control, be respected by their children, and be loved by them as well. Maintaining balance requires recognizing both extremes and working carefully on a consistent strategy of love and discipline. We will make many mistakes in this area, particularly when we are tired or under stress. Typically, many parents are overly strict with their first child and not strict enough with the last. New parents try hard and usually need to learn to relax, but we cannot afford to let down by the time the last child arrives, unconsciously permitting behavior that has not been allowed for our other children.

Sometimes we have to say to our children, "I didn't handle that in the right way, and I'm sorry. Will you forgive me?" In too many homes there is not enough allowance for failure on the part of children or parents. Allowing children to fail is important for their growth. If we cover up for or bail out our kids when they fail, they won't learn the consequences of their mistakes. When they make their own decisions and experience failure, it is our job to comfort them as they take whatever punishment comes or they make restitution. Nevertheless, we must help them to learn accountability for their actions and to understand the ramifications of future disobedience or failure.

Remember, God is bigger than all our failures. He can work through our mistakes and our sins to bring about his purposes. We are weak, fallible creatures, but we are in partnership with a great and mighty God. As we seek his help, he will enable our children to mature into fine men and women.

QUESTIONS FOR REFLECTION

1. Of the four types of parenting styles discussed in this chapter, which best describes you? Your spouse?
2. Are there areas in which your styles cause conflict in your marriage? Discuss one specific example of disagreement and agree on how you will handle this aspect of discipline the next time it occurs.
3. Discuss with your spouse (or with another parent) your goals for discipline in the home. How can you and other parents regularly support one another in matters of discipline?

Nothing is impossible with God.

Luke 1:37

II

Cultivating Faith
Susan with John

A parent's greatest privilege is to cultivate an atmosphere of authentic faith in God. Millennia ago an exhausted leader expressed a dramatic choice made on behalf of his family. Joshua was the leader of the children of Israel. Over the years, working alongside Moses, he had observed the fickleness of these people from the time they had been miraculously delivered from slavery in Egypt. Joshua had been chosen to lead a new generation of Jews into the Promised Land. Even now the Israelites still seemed incapable of deciding whether to trust in God. Joshua challenged these people, who were now his great extended family, in what was perhaps the most important speech of his career. He said: "Choose for yourselves this day whom you will serve, whether the gods your forefathers served beyond the River, or the gods of the Amorites, in whose land you are living. But as for me and my household, we will serve the LORD" (Josh. 24:15).

The first step toward building a Christian home is for the adults of the family to make the decision that growing together in relationship to God will be their top priority. Wherever the parents are in their own faith journey, they can make this decision, because God takes us right where we are. Our Lord is more concerned with our desire to grow in him than he is with our current understanding of him. In fact, even if one spouse is not at the place of being able to make this commitment, God will honor one parent who must take this step alone. However, the home will always be out of sync unless both husband and wife are committed to God's leadership in their home. Newlyweds or adults of any age can make this decision.

The parent's role is first to make the decision individually to become a follower of Christ and then to work toward leading the others in the home to follow him as a family. The Bible warns believers against marrying nonbelievers, but sometimes one will come into a true faith in Christ after having been married to a person who is not a committed Christian. In such cases God has promised, through Paul, that the family will be touched significantly. "The unbelieving husband has been sanctified through his wife, and the unbelieving wife has been sanctified through her believing husband. Otherwise your children would be unclean, but as it is, they are holy" (1 Cor. 7:14). Even if your mate doesn't yet know the Lord, you have the privilege and the authority to do all you can to raise your own children to become the Lord's.

Even before marriage the common decision should be made to entrust the marriage and any children to Christ. When two people share a common faith in Christ, they have a great head start in cultivating families of faith, but we should never feel that it is too late to make this important beginning.

Next, we must realize the importance of determining, with God's help, to be completely honest in all things, and particularly about our relationship with God, realizing that no children expect their parents to have all the answers. Children do not need perfect parents, but they do need honest parents.

Over the years we have watched the marriage and family life of Frank and Beth, a couple in our church. When their two oldest girls were five and nine, Frank and Beth experienced a deep sense of restlessness in their marriage. Frank, even though he was not a believer at that time, had come from a Christian background, and he had the sense that the family's problem was spiritual in nature. They had not felt the need for a faith up to this point, but now they seemed to stand on the brink of a period in which they needed either to discover genuine faith or they would perhaps see their family gradually disintegrate.

Just before they came to our church, Frank and Beth both came to faith in Jesus Christ as their Lord and Savior. They explained their salvation experience to their girls, who then also expressed the desire to ask Jesus Christ to come into their lives. The parents understood that this was a new beginning for the whole family, and that they had a lot to learn. They sought out a church to join, attended fellowship groups, read the Bible, and became deliberate about prayer. They discussed with their girls the things they were learning and, in all honesty, the things they did not understand. As time went by changes began to occur within the home. Without any pretense, the parents sought one another's forgiveness and their children's forgiveness when they hurt one another. The girls, responding to these positive changes in their parents, began to grow in their faith as well. Neither parent knew much about their newfound faith, and they made plenty of mistakes. But their children knew that what was happening was real. Raising kids with faith doesn't demand that the parents be completely mature or wise in their own faith. Raising children of faith simply means that their parents have a hunger to grow and are acting upon that hunger.

Should we put pressure on our children to believe in Christ? How old should they be before we begin talking to them about spiritual things? Many parents feel that pushing faith too hard or too soon might cause their children to rebel. They wonder what the right approach should be.

We believe the best approach is an honest and open one. We explained to our children individually when they were very young that God loves them and sent his Son, Jesus Christ, to show us how to live and to take away our sins on the cross. We explained that he wanted to be very close to them and, in fact, wanted to come into their hearts and live there forever as their friend and master. We explained to them Revelation 3:20, in which Christ is pictured standing at the door of our hearts knocking and waiting to be invited in.

We told our children that only they could make the decision to invite Christ into their lives, and we explained that this was something they would want to do at some point in their lives when they knew they were ready. In our home each of our five children had taken this step personally by the time he or she was four years of age, and each still has memories of this time. We wrote about it in their baby books so that they would have a clear remembrance.

None of our children has lived a perfect life or has always followed the Lord completely, nor have their parents. People who make decisions to follow Christ at an early age will certainly go through multiple times of commitment to him throughout their lives. But from the early years they will have had the blessing of knowing that God is with them and that he will never leave them. This provides a tremendous sense of security. The Holy Spirit has begun to work within their tender hearts from these early years, molding them into the people he has created them to be.

BAPTISM OF CHILDREN

All Christians receive their children as a gift of God, and believe they belong to God. But they express this truth differently. Most churches throughout history and throughout the world bring their children to be baptized. But many prefer to "dedicate" their children, postponing baptism until the children have themselves come to a personal belief in Jesus. We ourselves (John and Susan) believe that infant baptism is a biblical concept, and therefore it is this that we wish to elaborate on.

Holy baptism is a sacred action that takes place within the church symbolizing the deep and hidden reality of a person's life and that person's relationship with God. While many churches baptize infants, others don't baptize until the person has come to faith. If a person is baptized as an infant the sacrament has one meaning and if he is baptized as a young adult or older the meaning is somewhat different.

But whatever the age of the person being baptized, baptism is the birth rite of the worldwide Christian church. We know from our own experience that as we pass from certain states of experience to others some rite is often performed. An alien who comes into a country and becomes a citizen of that country participates in a particular rite of becoming a citizen. A civilian who joins the armed services participates in a rite of passage. The rite speaks both to the initiate and to the whole community.

In just the same way, when someone becomes a member of the church family, either by being born into a Christian home, or by deciding for himself at a later age to become a follower of Christ, a definite ceremony or rite is performed. This rite is baptism.

Jesus commanded his disciples to baptize others who had repented of their sins and accepted his good news and who sought to follow him. "Therefore go and make disciples of all nations, baptizing them in the name of the Father and of the Son and of the Holy Spirit, and teaching them to obey everything I have commanded you" (Matt. 28:19–20).

The disciples did this, baptizing both adults and whole families as well (Acts 16:33; 1 Cor. 1:16). This may mean that little children as well as adults were baptized in the earliest days of the church. We do know for certain that infant baptism was a common practice by the end of the second century.

The mere external rite of baptism does not bring about any magical change within the person baptized. The change occurs inside a person when, because of the Gospel and the work of the Holy Spirit, that person repents and believes in Jesus. Baptism does not provide a ticket to heaven. Only Jesus can ensure our acceptance into heaven, and he made that possible by dying for our sins on the cross. Let's be clear: Baptism does not make people Christians. It is rather a sacrament, that is an outward, visible, public dramatization of God's saving grace—in the case of adults, looking back to their conversion, in the case of children, looking forward to it in anticipation of coming to genuine faith.

When adults are baptized the baptism comes after a personal commitment to live for Christ. It is a public, sacramental demonstration of a prior fact, in the same way that Elizabeth II was crowned in Westminster Abby in June 1953 although she had actually been serving as queen for some months before the public rite of coronation took place.

When infants are baptized, the meaning is more complicated. How can a small child who has no apparent knowledge of Christ be baptized in order to symbolize a Christian commitment, which has already been made? He can't. Children are baptized, therefore, *prior* to and in anticipation of the person's decision to follow Christ, just as adults are baptized *after* this decision.

Why do we do this? Children are God's most precious gift to parents. We know that God cares deeply for little children. We find an intense interest and concern for children in the biblical stories of Moses, Samuel, Isaiah, John, and many others. In fact, the Son of God himself became a tiny child in order to show his care for us.

As God cares for children, so do we, and we want the very best for our children, in the spiritual realm as well as in the material. We want our child from the very first to enter into a relationship with God that will last forever. Should we shut children out of the church just because they are too young to exhibit a faith in Christ? No, we bring them into the church from the earliest days and in many of our churches we do this through the entry rite of infant baptism as the beginning of their child-like relationship to God, who is the Lord of their family. This is in *anticipation* of their own future personal decision to follow the God of their fathers.

God himself initiated this concept with Abraham, father of the Jewish people, through the rite of circumcision. From the time of Abraham on, infants were admitted as members of the Jewish community by this public act that signified their inclusion in the covenant God made with Abraham and his descendants. Abraham himself was circumcised as an adult because of his faith in God, but Isaac and his descendants were circumcised as infants in *anticipation* of their faith. During the whole period of time from Abraham to Christ (fifteen hundred years or more) God accepted children into his family on the basis of their parents' faith. Then, when the child reached an appropriate age and was taught the things of God, he made his own personal decision to follow God, and he was accepted as a member of the Jewish family.

This was the recognized rule in the day of Jesus, and since he did not teach otherwise, many have concluded that it applies to the Christian church as well. This circumcision in the Old Testament and baptism in the New Testament was the sign of covenant relationship recognizing that the child has been born into a believing family. This is a simple explanation of our New Testament foundation for infant baptism, and it is the view that has been taken by the majority of Christians down through the ages, although many Christians opt to wait until their children have come to personal faith before they are baptized.

Christ's attitude toward children was one of affection, concern, and gentleness. He did not refuse them his blessing, but rather purposefully laid his hands in blessing on what must have been countless little ones during the years of his ministry. The significance of this cannot be overstated. They were capable of receiving the blessing no matter how young they were (Mark 10:13–16). In the Book of Acts there are two prominent stories of entire families being baptized in the early church (Acts

16:15, 31–33). Paul addresses little children in Christian families in such a way as to suggest that they are already included in the church (Eph. 6:1; Col. 3:20).

It is our belief that baptism for an infant is somewhat akin to the planting of a seed in good soil. It is an action performed in faith that, one day, what is now being begun by the parents will be completed by the child himself. It is clearly inappropriate for a child to be baptized when neither parent is a believer. It is not reasonable to expect that parents who make no profession of Christianity could bring their children up as Christians and lead them to an adult personal decision for Christ.

Christian parents present their child before the church, dedicating themselves to the Christian nurture of the child and dedicating the child to God. The gathered church accepts the infant as a new member and acknowledges its own responsibility to help in the Christian nurture of the child.

The roads that different children move along in coming to adult Christian faith are different for each individual. Both of us were raised in deeply committed and loving Christian homes. I (John) can never remember a time when I did not have a strong faith in Christ and a close relationship with him. Susan, however, in a very similar home, grew up without the assurance of that close relationship with Christ. She says that she did not have assurance of Christ being in her life until she made a personal adult decision at about age twenty to invite Jesus Christ into her life to be her Master and Savior. She had gone to church, prayed, and attended Sunday school, but the certainty of knowing Jesus personally was not there.

Your children will travel different roads however their baptisms occur and their faith develops. Baptism in no way guarantees that the child will grow up to be a believing Christian. However, it is the first step, and it is a privilege to be able to take that step.

OUR NEED FOR GOD'S HELP

As a parent your responsibility is to be certain that your own relationship with God is as it should be. Successful parenting is difficult in our culture. We need God's help. The Lord Jesus stands ready to come into our lives and give us the strength and wisdom we need to be the parents we should want to be. As you meditate on these things, you may want to make the following prayer your own.

> *Dear God, I thank you for the child you have given me. I thank you for the love you have for me as well as for my precious child. I need your help. I have turned too often from you and pursued my own ways. I confess my sins and humbly ask for your forgiveness. I open the door of my life and ask your Son, Jesus, to come in as the Savior who died for me. I pray that he will be with me to guide and strengthen me. I want to be the person and parent you created me to be. These things I pray through Jesus Christ our Lord. Amen.*

Some parents feel that by participating in church school, children receive all the specifically Christian teaching they need. But the amount of time that church school teachers have with children is quite small. Probably no more than 1 percent of a child's time is spent in church school class. Wise Sunday school teachers attempt to teach the Bible and its relevance to students, but they realize that their most lasting influence will probably be as a role model. I expect that my son will long remember his rugby-playing, soccer-enthusiast third-grade Sunday school teacher because of that man's joyous enthusiasm for Christ, for life, and for sport more than for his expositions of the parables. I can't, for instance, remember a thing one Sunday school teacher taught me during the two years I had her as a teacher, but I will never forget how her faith in the Lord sustained her when her son was killed in a freak accident.

Surely some Sunday school teachers are effectively able to teach certain aspects of the faith to our children. But that responsibility is largely ours. Therefore, family prayers and Bible study and discussions about the vast scope of life and what it means to be a Christian must be an integral part of our children's growing up years.

Commitment to Christ is a progressive thing that matures all through our lives. A five-year-old can love Jesus sincerely and be as obedient to what he understands of Jesus' demands for discipleship as can a fifty-year-old Christian leader. But as a child grows older, he must continue to re-affirm his commitment to Christ as his horizons, his abilities, his opportunities, and his temptations ever broaden.

A GROWING DEPENDENCE ON THE FATHER

As we raise our children in the Christian faith, our goal as parents must be that of steadily turning our children from dependence on us to dependence on their heavenly Father. We are with them for approximately eighteen years, but he is with them for eternity. So how do we bring about this growing maturity and shifting of dependence? There are at least five components that will help us become more dependent on God ourselves and will help our children grow in faith and dependence on God over the years: God's Word, prayer, fellowship, vision, and worship.

The Importance of God's Word

One of the greatest legacies we can pass on to our children is a knowledge of the Scriptures, a familiarity with the stories, promises, and principles found in the Bible. Wise parents will seek out Bible storybooks prepared especially to be read to children from the earliest years and will develop a discipline of reading Bible stories to their children on a daily basis. Many find bedtime to be the best time for this, while others have found that breakfast time, after school, or some other time works well for them. If you are finding it difficult to read together on a daily basis, set aside a specific time every week for a family Bible study. With small children it should be short. Give children a Bible of their own—a little picture Bible before they learn to read—and then a children's version when they are learning to read. Let them learn one promise by heart and underline it in their Bible. As the children grow older, you can select a passage and, after reading it silently, let each person share what he or she has discovered in reading it.

Family vacations will provide a more relaxed time to have Bible study together. One summer while we were at the beach for a week, we studied many of the great biblical sea passages. Since the children were between the ages of eleven and eighteen at the time, we were able to do individual study. My (Susan) husband chose one story and one psalm that had something to do with water. We separated for individual quiet times and then returned for a time of sharing.

After we had read about a sea storm described in Psalm 107:23–32, one of our daughters, reflecting on verse 28, wrote, "There are some times that the Lord frees me from my distress and I just take it for granted." How honest young people are!

On another evening, after studying the story of Jonah, we experienced a thunderstorm that blew up over the ocean. Watching the lightning blaze and hearing the roar of angry surf in the black night made Jonah's predicament come alive in a most dramatic way. One of the twins said, "Wow! Now I know why Jonah was scared."

Creatively taking advantage of opportunities to introduce the Word of God to our small children will instill in them a hunger to initiate their own personal study as they reach the teen years. When they get older take them to a Christian bookstore to pick out a devotional book to guide their quiet times.

Our children's hunger for God's Word will grow as they observe our hunger. If they see us spending time reading the Bible, they will want to also. If I want to become a person of faith and desire the same for my children, I must make a priority of spending time alone each day in the Scriptures and in prayer. Raising children who have a love for the Bible occurs as parents themselves take time to learn from God's Word.

Prayer

The most effective way to teach our children the importance of prayer is to pray with them. Sometimes we hesitate to pray with them because of two common fears.

Many of us fear that, because of our own unworthiness, we cannot pray, since there is so much in our lives that is not as it should be. But we must remember that God is our heavenly Father and desires to communicate with us. He already knows everything in our lives yet still desires to talk with us and listen to us. And so we go to God, not because of who we are, but because of who he is.

A second fear parents commonly face is, "What if God doesn't answer? Won't that damage my child's faith?" God answers prayer in three basic ways: "Yes," "No," and "Wait." There may be a long silence when God answers with "Wait." "Wait" is hard for us to take, but we must remember that God is not operating according to our timetable. He is not limited to working in ways that we can predict. He always does what is best, not necessarily what is fast.

When God answers our prayers with a "no," he answers in that way out of love because he knows what is best for us in just the same way a parent would say no, for example, if a young child wanted to leave on a long trip alone. Often we don't understand God's answers, but we need to remember that God can be trusted and that he always answers based on his love for us. When we explain to our children the different ways God answers our prayers, they will be assured that they can talk to God about anything.

Try to establish a regular prayer time as a family. For many years we have kept beside our breakfast table a large bulletin board covered with photos of friends who live outside our hometown. Each morning for years our custom has been to have one member of the family be the prayer leader of the day who will pray for someone whose picture is on the bulletin board. Also, over breakfast, different family members share what they are facing that day. One child may have a test in school; another may have a meeting that he or she is concerned about. After a brief time of prayer, we then go our separate ways.

Sometimes, over the years, we have used a prayer notebook to record special things for which we were praying as well as how and when we saw God answer those prayers. Looking back over the years, the many ways God has answered prayer have become evident. Keeping such a notebook reminds us of God's faithfulness and encourages us to believe that he will also answer our current prayers.

These regularly scheduled, planned prayer times will differ in each family. The important thing is to look at your schedule and determine when you can have time to pray together. However, we should also pray spontaneously as the need arises.

Sometimes we are made aware of a situation and think, "I'll pray about that later," and then we forget. Decide now to pray on the spot when needs come up in the home. When we pray as needs arise, the spontaneity of our prayers illustrates the relevancy of our faith, and it teaches our children how dependent we are on God moment by moment.

To maintain creativity in our prayers, it helps to distinguish between short-range, medium-range, and long-range prayers. A short-range prayer would be for your child's basketball game this weekend—that he would have fun, do well, and be kept safe. A medium-range prayer would be for your high school senior's college choice. Long-range prayers concern things so far off that we do not know when they will be answered. Praying for a friend to come to faith in Christ might be a long-range prayer. We just keep praying.

We must never underestimate the power of prayer. The Son of God himself found it necessary to pray to his Father in heaven about many things over and over again. Wise parents will not limit family prayers only to family matters; they will pray for neighbors, the community, the nation, and worldwide concerns. One small child's prayer may, in some way understood only to God, have great impact.

Fellowship

The presence of close friends who love us and encourage us is vitally important to our own personal growth and maturity. This is true also for our children. We can't make it alone. We need one another.

For many years John and I have maintained a close relationship with two other married couples, Larry and Betsy and Bob and Elaine. Living in three different places, widely separated, we decided years ago to make a priority of being together at least once a year, and for years we have spent one special weekend in the mid-winter together, usually meeting at our farmhouse in the Virginia countryside.

Leaving the children at home, we head for the farm for our weekend of refreshment. We spend many long hours curled up in front of the fire talking. The men chop wood and do chores together, and the women go shopping for bargains in the village. During our time together, each of us takes a turn sharing what is happening in our lives personally. We ask one another tough questions about how our marriages are going, about our relationships with our children, about the ways we are spending our money, and about the priorities we are teaching our children. There are always both laughter and tears during these gatherings. We love one another, exalt one another, encourage one another, and hold one another accountable. These relationships have been built over thirty years and are crucially important for each of us because we have learned that to become people of faith, we must have friends who will encourage us and hold us accountable.

This is one of the reasons why Jesus pulled together the disciples into a special relationship with himself and with one another. People who try to follow Christ without the ongoing, close friendship of other believers are likely to fall away from God. As we make the time to develop close relationships with other believers, our children receive blessings. They will have a group of adults whom they know and who love and care for them. There have been times in our children's lives when they needed to hear things from an adult who is not their parent, and they have heard these things from Bob and Elaine or Larry and Betsy. Our children view these other families as an extension of our own family. Also, they catch the vision that the Christian life is not meant to be lived alone as they see our relationship with close Christian friends. It is interesting to us how our children and the children of our friends have forged deep and lasting relationships over the years. Two of our daughters have roomed together in college, and four of our sons have developed close friendships, spending much time with one another even though they attended different universities. These children have established a lifelong commitment to one another.

Our children need Christian friends of their own. This is why we have encouraged them to be involved in the youth group at our church or in parachurch organizations that pull kids together for fellowship, mission work, Bible study, and worship. One of our sons invited a number of young men with whom he was in a Bible study at our church all through his adolescent years to serve as groomsmen in his wedding. These young men consistently make time to be together. They play together and pray together, cherishing one another as friends and as brothers in Christ.

Perhaps you desire to have a few close friends like this. God knows this desire. Ask him to show you two or three people to whom you can be committed. Begin praying now for your children to develop these kinds of relationships as they grow up.

A Sense of Vision

Periodically certain families come along who impact the life of a nation. They seem to have gained from one another and their forebears a sense of destiny or purpose in serving their nation. They are people of vision who are committed to making an impact on other people. Somewhere along the line, some parents communicated a powerful vision. The Nehru-Gandhi family have been leaders in India for decades, and younger Gandhis seem to be coming along. Theodore Roosevelt, Franklin Roosevelt, and Winston Churchill were all cousins. Over the years a strong vision for public service and great leadership was imparted in that family, just as is true of the Bush family in the United States. Families like this show us that we need to have a vision for our families.

Ambition can be a negative characteristic as sometimes it is self-seeking and ruthless. But Christ commends the ambition of putting our gifts to work in his service. In our Lord's parable of the talents, the master commends the ambitious servant and is clearly disgusted with the cautious one who only wanted to play it safe. We want our children to make a significant impact on their world for the sake of Christ. How then can we instill in them a sense of holy ambition? Can we help them develop a passion for a Christlike life and a vision for their own personal ministry without playing God in their lives?

The answer is yes. First, of course, we must pray for our children, asking God to begin to show us the unique gifts he has given to each of them. As we gain some idea of our children's potential, we encourage them and dream with them about the many ways in which God might use their gifts. One child may have a gift of leadership, while another may have an unusual capacity for compassion. One may have superior academic potential, while another may have strong athletic ability. A young man from our church once visited one of our sons who was ill at the time. This fellow told our son that he had been praying for him and had been given a strong sense that God was going to use our son one day to lead many others to Christ, and he wanted him to know that. That certainly made an impact on this young boy.

Developing a sense of destiny in our children will spur them on. Study your children. Encourage them to develop their gifts or to pursue a particular interest and use it to help others. One of our main responsibilities as parents is to be alert to the unique ways in which God has made our children and to encourage them in the positive use of their gifts. We should not, however, try to determine their professions or vocations. God is the one who calls our children to this or that work as a way of life.

Reading biographies to our young children and encouraging them to read stories of heroes and particularly heroes of the faith will give them a sense of the way God works through his people. Many schools have reading lists for children. We parents would do well to put together similar reading lists for our own children. Not only do they need to be enriched by the example of heroes whom they learn about through books and videos, but they also need to have exposure to role models in daily life. Take every opportunity to have people visit your home who exhibit the kinds of qualities you want to be developed in your children. Many a child's destiny has been impacted by simple dinner table conversation.

Use summer vacation time as an opportunity for the spiritual enrichment of your children. Many push their young people to work hard at jobs during the summer to earn money. This is often necessary and legitimate, but we need to ask ourselves if our child will benefit more from the extra money for a new bicycle or automobile or from involvement in a summer mission trip or two weeks at a Christian camp. Summers have been a crucial time for our children's spiritual growth. Many times our children have been enriched by exposure to believers in situations where neither of us was present. When your children hear other spiritual leaders communicate biblical truths, they may be more receptive to them than they would be hearing them from you. Make wise use of your children's summers. Opportunities abound for spiritual enrichment.

Vital Worship

Regular corporate worship with the church family is an important part of our life with God. The church is Christ's creation, and however imperfect it is, it plays an important role in his purposes for our world. It is our spiritual family. It is composed of people of all ages, races, backgrounds, and interests. It is a community that ministers to us from birth to death, providing continuity from one generation to the next.

Staying away from church and staying home or pursuing leisure outings on Sunday can become easy, but we really do need the church and we really do need worship. We need to be meeting with the whole body of Christ to worship and praise God. Our children need to be a part of something that includes believers of all ages and backgrounds and lasts longer than this Bible club or that youth activity.

Worship is not always stimulating for us or for our children. We may have the idea that worship is for us and that if it does not give us warm feelings and happy thoughts, it is not effective. Worship should certainly connect with us emotionally and intellectually, but worship is not primarily for us. It is first and foremost for God, who desires, requests, and expects our adoration, praise, and attention. God, in fact, inhabits the praise of his people (Ps. 22:3 KJV). Something very special takes place as the body of Christ comes together weekly to praise God, to pray to God, to listen to his Word, and to be challenged and comforted. Worship lifts us up out of ourselves and reminds us of who God is. Adoration is a truly unselfish experience.

But what about the child who says, "Church is just boring, Mom"? Most children will say that at some point, but I'm hard pressed to discern where boredom is found to be wrong. In fact, there is nothing wrong with being bored every so often.

School can be boring, yet when our children complain, we don't allow them to skip school, because we know it's important. When we allow our children to skip church but not school, we are communicating that school is more important than church. As children, my husband and I were both expected to be in church on Sundays. Both of us often found it to be somewhat boring and felt it was a waste of time, but we had no choice. We went. In college we were not as frequent in our attendance for a time. But both of us found, in our own ways, that the old hymns and prayers we had unconsciously memorized in our youth came back to us bringing comfort and joy. We began to realize what we had missed by not being regularly involved in worship. When so many things are changing in our lives, we find comfort in being in church on Sunday, where we are reminded that we are a part of a worldwide family in Christ. Worship reminds us that we are a part of something so much greater than just those gathered in a particular building, for all over the world people are meeting to worship the same God.

When we make a priority of worship as a family, it communicates to our children that all of us are willing to set aside our own time in order to come together with other believers and join in praise to God. This tells our children that we understand that the almighty God is much more important than we are.

Worship, vision, fellowship, prayer, the Scriptures—all these things are important ingredients for growing in faith. Becoming a family of faith is a journey in which all of us are involved. We must not wait until we "achieve" maturity and then teach our children. We will never "arrive" ourselves, for we are always people in process. But as we honestly share our own experience of God and our journey of faith with our children, we will be growing together in the goodness and greatness of God and in the awareness of our constant need for him in our lives.

QUESTIONS FOR REFLECTION

1. How important is it to you that your children know and love God?
2. Do you think your children could articulate God's plan of salvation? Do you know if your children have personally asked Christ to come into their lives?
3. What plans do you have to help your children grow in their relationship with Christ over the next year? What resources will you take advantage of?

"My Spirit, who is on you, and my words that I have put in your mouth will not depart from your mouth, or from the mouths of your children, or from the mouths of their descendants from this time on and forever," says the LORD.

Isaiah 59:21

12

Parents and Adolescents
Susan

Every parent of a teenager knows that the adolescent years are full of surprises and challenges. These young people, who are no longer children but not yet adults, often confuse themselves as well as everyone around them with their sudden mood shifts and various attempts at expressing their individuality. Sometimes the only explanation for a teenager's behavior is just "adolescence." These are the best of times and the worst of times with our children. They are years full of opportunities and rewards. One word summarizes the season of adolescence for both young people and for their parents—*awkward*.

THE AWKWARD TEEN

The teenage years are awkward for our children in a number of ways. Four of the primary problem areas are physical changes, emotional fragility, social adjustment, and spiritual confusion.

149

Physical Changes

Young people want very much to grow up physically, but the changes that come often do not seem to come in the way the kids want them to. They develop either too early or too late. If a boy's voice changes late, it can be agonizingly embarrassing. If a girl needs a bra too early, she can feel ill at ease. Pimples can lead to dramatic despair for both girls and boys. Hormones are unpredictable. We have to help our young people understand that their bodies are simply going through a major time of physical readjustment, which is difficult for a while but eventually will be complete.

Emotional Fragility

Adolescence is also awkward emotionally. Little things that don't seem to matter to an adult tend to be quite upsetting to teenagers who are afraid of being embarrassed. Teenagers live in fear of standing out. If their shoes are not the kind that are currently popular among their peers, they feel inferior. As parents we need to learn to be sensitive to how our own behavior can cause our children to be embarrassed. For instance, Dad's whistling while walking down the street can be annoying to the sensitive teenager. Or his putting his arm around his son as they walk through a shop can be uncomfortable. Anything that is not cool or that is in the least bit out of the norm among their peers can upset teenagers greatly. They find themselves in two positions. On the one hand, they still want to be children and to be cared for, whereas on the other hand they desperately want to be independent and mature. It is no surprise then that their emotions and behavior alternate radically between these two extremes. One minute the daughter wants to crawl up in her dad's lap, and the next minute she insists that she doesn't need any help in making her own decisions. Parents often feel like they are walking on eggshells trying to anticipate what their adolescent child's needs and reactions might be.

Social Adjustment

Friends are very important during the teen years because they help our children define who they are. Many teenagers begin to spend inor-dinate amounts of time talking on the telephone as a way of strengthening their social relationships. Sometimes our children almost seem to be trying on different personality types to find the one that fits them best. One day your daughter may be the life of the party, talking all the time, and the next she may be extremely quiet and withdrawn. Your son may be a tough guy one day and enormously funny and outgoing the next. Teens alternate between ways of expressing themselves, because they're really not sure who they are. This, of course, is tremendously exhausting to parents who are trying to keep up with their child and to siblings who are constantly adjusting to the unpredictable nature of living with a teenager. The fact is, these things are also frustrating to the child who isn't sure who he or she really wants to be.

Spiritual Confusion

Often adolescence is awkward spiritually as well, because children need to learn to shift their dependence from the faith of their parents to a much more personal dependence on God. Such a shift usually involves some questioning of their faith as a part of the process, and it is not at all uncommon for teenagers to think to themselves, *Why should I believe what I've been taught? That may be good enough for my parents, but I'm not sure it satisfies me.* Such doubt and uncertainty, struggling through to one's own faith, is an indispensable part of growing up. Adults who have never gone through this process often retain a childish faith throughout their lives. Parents need to be extremely patient and prayerful during this time.

THE AWKWARD PARENT

The teenage years are not just awkward for teens, they are awkward for parents as well for a number of reasons. So many of our parental assumptions and policies suddenly do not seem applicable, and it's not unusual for us to experience insecurity over whether we're making wise decisions on behalf of our children. We constantly question whether we're handling a particular challenge the right way. We worry about whether our children will rebel. We wonder exactly what they are thinking, because often they shut down communication with us and it's difficult for us to get them to open up again. There are many unknowns during this time, because, try as we might, we cannot completely under-

151

stand what is going on in their lives, and now that they are getting older, the stakes seem to be much higher.

As our young people begin to develop their own viewpoints, they tend to argue with us. We need maturity to recognize that our children are in the process of weaning themselves away from us and becoming their own persons. This process causes us to feel that we are losing control. Even though the toddler years were tremendously exhausting for us, in many ways the teenage years are just as exhausting. The difference is that it tends to be an emotional exhaustion rather than the physical exhaustion of those young years.

Our judgment as parents is frequently being questioned. We wonder what is realistic to expect from our young people and what disciplines we should maintain. We consider what things we must insist on and what things we are willing to release.

As we realize the shortness of time we will have our children with us, we know that we must let them go more and more. But it is difficult, because we know that they do not yet have the adult judgment necessary to make wise decisions. We are moving from the nurturing phase toward the launching phase, and it is not easy for most parents. The children want to be released, yet we know that they are not ready. We often feel inadequate ourselves.

GIFTS YOU CAN GIVE

In spite of the awkwardness of the teen years, they can be a wonderful time in the life of parents and children. This is the time when our friendships with our children can go much deeper and we can begin to relate to them as adults. We can talk with them about things we never could discuss with them before, and we can dream with them about the future.

As we move through the teen years, there are a number of specific gifts we can give to our children that can enable the development of mature, lifelong friendships with them. We will look at these in the remainder of this chapter.

Giving Them Time

Wise parents of teenagers will try simply to be around their kids. This doesn't have to be highly organized. It can be as simple as plopping down on your teenage daughter's bed and chatting about her day before dinner or kicking around a soccer ball with your son in the yard. It can involve thumbing through a clothing catalog with your daughter or going to a ball game or to the movies. Giving your child time is a way of saying, "I like you; I want to be with you. You are special to me." Most of us are quite busy, but if we allow our busyness to keep us from being with our teenagers, we miss the opportunity to communicate with them. It is difficult to orchestrate in advance an in-depth conversation with your teenager, but it is certain that those kinds of conversations will not occur unless you are available to your kids. Plan ways to be with them.

One of our friends has two sons who are in a band. From the parents' perspective the music is awful. It is not in the least appealing to them. But the dad always helps them get to their concerts and is there throughout as a way of saying, "If this is important to you, it's important to me." Another of our friends and his teenage son decided to participate with a group in our town that feeds hungry street people. So on many nights you'll find father and son working together in the soup kitchen where they are not only caring for the poor, but also building a partnership in caring for the needy. They are developing a sense of compassion as well as strengthening their friendship. There is no substitute for time spent together.

Showing Them Respect

One of the surprises in raising teenagers is how many times they develop a thoughtful perspective and have wise discernment in various areas of life. We begin to realize that they are maturing, and *we* can learn from *them*. The parent who always tells and never asks misses an opportunity to grow.

Asking our teens' ideas about different things communicates to them that we are interested in knowing what they think, that their perspective is valuable to us. We won't always agree with their viewpoint, but respecting them and wanting to hear their ideas communicates love and appreciation. If we are always correcting their opinions, we are communicating that we don't respect what they are thinking. Even if their opinions are superficial, it is still important for us to hear and appreciate them.

One summer at a Canadian camp for families, we spoke to parents about family life. Near the end of the week we decided that it would be helpful to hear from some of the teenagers, so we asked our two teenage sons as well as a couple of teenage girls who were at the camp to form a panel to speak to the parents. We asked their thoughts about how parents of teenagers could do a better job. One of the young people told us how important it is to give teenagers a positive reputation: "Stop talking about the teenage years as being awful years that are simply to be endured." Another one said: "You don't necessarily need to expect that your teenagers will rebel. In fact, my parents expected me not to rebel, and I haven't."

Telling our children repeatedly how grateful and proud we are to be their parents lets them know that we respect and admire them. Many parents groan and complain when they talk about the teenage years, and they seem to expect their teenagers to give them great difficulty. Many times this is the case, but it certainly doesn't have to be that way. When teens feel they have to live up to the bad reputation with which they have been tagged, they may very well pursue that reputation vigorously. Focus on the positive, look for the things your teenagers do well, commend them over and over again. We need to do this in order to balance out the necessary correcting that also must go on during the teen years.

Creating a Positive Attitude toward the Future

Because of all the rapid changes our young people experience, and because of the elevated need for approval and acceptance during the teenage years, adolescents are sometimes prone to despair. They need to know that in time things will get better.

When I was about thirteen I was convinced that I would never have any friends. My teeth were crooked, I wore thick glasses, and my body seemed terribly different from the way my friends' looked. I can still remember what an encouragement it was to me when, after a fit of tears, my mother put her arms around me and said, "Susan, I remember feeling the same way." She told me stories of how she felt when she was my age. Then she said something very important: "Your turn will come. You will be pretty, and you will have friends." She gave me hope and helped me to see that it was normal to feel the way I did. Remembering this helped me to see how important it was to pass this hope on to my own daughters when they were about the same age.

The promise from God to the Jews when they were experiencing a painful period of exile brings great hope to us as well. "'For I know the plans I have for you,' declares the LORD, 'plans to prosper you and not to harm you, plans to give you hope and a future'" (Jer. 29:11). This is a good Bible verse to write out and put on your teenager's mirror. You might want to add a personal note telling her that you are certain that God has a very special plan for her. Tell her you are honored to be her parent and that you have confidence in her. You might try to envision for your child a picture of hope for the future as you describe some of her fine qualities. Perhaps you might say something like this:

> My dear daughter, you are unusually creative. The positive side of this gift is that you have a great imagination and you will be a great problem solver. You probably won't get bored very easily. A negative side to this gift is that you have a tendency to worry. It helps to recognize the weakness that comes with each gift. I know that God is going to use your creativity in a wonderful way to enrich many lives. It's a very special gift, and you are a very special young lady.

Frustration and disappointment crowd into teenagers' lives, and because circumstances seem more important during this season, teenagers sometimes feel that a particular problem is going to ruin their life. Of course, in time and with perspective these things will not be nearly as significant. Wise parents have to try to understand the agonizing impact of the disappointment of the moment and, at the same time, reassure their children that eventually this problem will not matter as much as it does right now.

Not being accepted at the particular school he or she desperately wanted to attend, being excluded from a very important outing, or losing a girlfriend or a boyfriend—these things can be very hard for our teenagers. What they need from us as parents is reassurance that conveys, "I know this is hard, very hard. But I'm not worried about it, because I know that in the end God is going to work things out." Romans 8:28 is a wonderful promise to claim during difficult times: "God works for the good of those who love him, who have been called according to his purpose."

Teenagers who are feeling uncertain about themselves and about their circumstances don't need parents who are easily upset as well. They need parents who communicate with empathy, objectivity, and a sense of humor! These can help restore a healthy perspective.

Appreciating Their Friends

Parents who create the kind of home atmosphere that encourages their children to want to bring their friends home with them are wise. Think of things you can do to make your home a fun place for your children and their peers. Do your best to have plenty of good food on hand, because teenagers are always hungry. Putting up a basketball hoop in the backyard was one of the best things my husband did, because it gave us an entertaining way of interacting with our kids and their friends in a sport we all enjoyed.

One of the most significant purchases I ever made cost very little but paid terrific dividends over a period of several years. I bought a second-hand table tennis table at a garage sale. This table made our home a fun teenage center, because our kids loved playing table tennis in the garage. Now that our kids are older, they still talk enthusiastically about the countless happy hours they spent with their friends around that old green table.

Something else that will attract young people is an atmosphere in which they are cared for. If we really take an interest in our children's friends, they will sense our love for them and will want to spend time in our homes. Getting to know these young people has been not only enlightening but also frequently quite encouraging as many times we are able to serve as a sounding board and friendly model to our children's friends.

One of my sons once said to me, "Mom, it's important for Joe to come over to our house. He doesn't get a lot of encouragement from his parents, and he just needs to come over here." Having been alerted, I went out of my way to talk to Joe and to get to know him. In the process I realized that I had learned some important principles from my son, who had taught me to spend time with his friends, to be interested, to ask them questions and draw them out, to care for them, and even to encourage and cheer for them.

We will not always know what subjects to talk about when we are with our children's friends, so it's helpful to ask our kids what their pals are most interested in. Teenagers can be intimidating, and you may feel inadequate in communicating with them. Ask your children for ideas, and they will give you good advice.

Sometimes you may find that you do not like your child's friends, and you must be careful in this situation. Go out of your way to get to know them, and you may discover that they are not as bad as you thought. On the other hand, you may find your concerns confirmed. Teenagers are quite loyal in their friendships, and it can be tricky talking to them about the reasons why you have some questions about their friendship with a certain person. It's important to see their friends in the best light possible, but if you find that your teenager is developing a significant relationship with peers who are negatively impacting your child, you will want to discuss this with a counselor, teacher, or another more experienced adult. These are opportunities for you and your mate to pray for wisdom. Younger teenagers often change friends very quickly, and the problem may take care of itself. But this isn't always the case. You may have to limit the time your child spends with others who are having a negative influence on him.

Giving Your Children Parameters

Teenagers need parameters and they need freedom. We must be careful in deciding where to stand firm and where to relax. One of the funniest things that happened during our sons' teenage years was an incident involving an old sofa. Late one night they came in from a night out with their friends, dragging into the house and up the steps into their room the filthiest couch we had ever seen. Our sons shared the same small bedroom, and there was hardly any unused space. They had decided they had to have this old sofa for their room and picked it up off the street where it had been discarded for trash collection. I could hardly imagine having such a filthy piece of furniture in our house.

"What are you doing with that?" I asked.

"It's our new couch," John responded, full of excitement. "I found it on the street during a treasure hunt. Someone put it out for trash, but I thought it would be perfect for our room."

"But it's filthy," I said, "and probably full of germs. There's no telling what kind of diseases you may pick up from that thing, and it doesn't even have cushions! You absolutely cannot put that awful thing in your room."

157

At that my son said in a serious voice but with laughter in his eye, "Mom, look at it like this. This is my teenage rebellion. Be grateful."

I realized at that point that he had me. After all, it was just a dirty couch. The boys moved the couch into their already crowded bedroom, where it stayed for many years as a memorial to our sons' "rebellion." As long as it remained there, it reminded us of an important principle: Learn to distinguish between the critical issues and the negotiable issues.

Although the sofa was ugly, it really did not represent an issue on which I needed to take a strong stand. It was something I needed to relax about. My decision about it was in no way vital to our son's character, and I realized that even though my sanitary instincts told me I did not want it in my house, I knew on the other hand that if they covered it with clean sheets, it probably wouldn't be too unbearable.

As teenagers express their independence in various ways, we have to have the wisdom to know how to let them do that. If, on the other hand, they are being disobedient or violating family policies, we have to take a firm stand.

Mom and Dad need to agree on what the crucial issues are in the family and explain these things clearly and consistently to the kids. Teenagers need to hear the "why" of family policies and not just the "what." They certainly will not always agree, but if they can absorb the reasoning behind our decisions, it will help them to understand that we are not just being stubborn. They may think we are being unreasonable, but at least they will recognize why we take the position we do. This is important for developing young adults. We have to be consistent in these matters and not be swayed by manipulation tactics. "No" means "no" and not "maybe." A teen will see through a parent who changes his or her position from situation to situation.

During our children's teenage years we always had clearly defined curfews for their returning home at night. We never allowed them to be home alone with a member of the opposite sex. We always insisted that they let us know where they would be and with whom. If their plans changed or for some reason they were going to be late in coming in, they knew they must call. The same rule applied to us as parents. We always let our children know if we were going to be later than we expected.

We did not allow our high school children to attend movies with a "Restricted" rating unless Dad had seen the movie himself or talked to someone he respected to get an opinion as to whether it was appropriate. Nor did we allow our children to watch television on school nights once the evening news was over except for a rare occasion such as a championship ball game.

Teenagers will argue with their parents over these policies, because they rarely believe they have enough freedom. But they do need and even want guidelines, even though they may not acknowledge it. Guidelines communicate to them that we care deeply about them.

If we have been firm with our children during their early years, generally the teen years will be less difficult. Many parents seem to do just the opposite. Some are very relaxed when the children are young and then impose strict guidelines when they get into the teen years. Teenagers need greatly to have parameters, but they must experience a gradual lessening of rules and an increasing freedom to make their own decisions to prepare for adulthood.

Being Understanding

I remember when a friend of one of our sons was very upset because he had just learned that he had failed his high school Spanish class. He had worked hard, trying his best, but had found learning a new language extremely difficult. When his dad learned about his son's failure, he responded with unusual wisdom by putting his arms around his son and saying, "Son, I don't know if I've ever told you this, but when I was in law school I failed one of my courses too." That word of empathy was a great comfort to his son. When the boy's parents met with his teacher and they made arrangements to hire a tutor to help him improve his grade, it communicated to the boy that they understood and were willing to work *with* him through this difficult time.

Two of our children expressed this idea of parents working with their children when I asked them on separate occasions what they thought teenagers needed from their parents. One of them said teenagers needed *teamwork*, and the other said they needed *partnership*. I found it interesting that their responses were similar even though they did not know what the other had said. When we communicate to teenagers that we understand, they feel that we are on the same team and are pulling together as partners in life in good times as well as bad. Many times John and I have shared with our children difficult personal situations that we were experiencing and have asked them to pray for us to have wisdom in knowing how to handle these situations. As we are willing to be open about our own difficulties and faults, we encourage a deeper friendship with our children that is built on understanding.

GIVING OUR CHILDREN OTHER ADULT FRIENDS

One of the greatest gifts we can give our children is the privilege of sharing in friendships with adults who are close friends of ours and who have the potential to become good friends with our children as well. Friendships with adults other than one's parents are extremely important in providing models and counsel for our young people.

Over the years it has not been at all unusual for our children to seek out our friends to talk with them about a particular problem. They have special relationships with their godparents and with several other friends of ours. If you alert them, some of your adult friends will be happy to take a special interest in and build friendships with your children. Our neighbor Holly often asked our younger daughters to take care of her baby to enable her to get some housework done. As she worked around the house, she made a habit of visiting with our girls, talking about friends, school, and other "girl stuff." Adult friends like this can have a great impact on your children if they share the same values as yours and reinforce what you are trying to teach them in the home. Often, because of their own experiences, they can give counsel in certain areas that may be better than your own, and teenagers sometimes receive such counsel much better from other trustworthy adults than from their own parents.

One of our neighbors wrote a letter to our son after he had spoken out in a public meeting about a certain school program. It had taken courage, because he had taken an unpopular stand. Our neighbor wrote him to encourage him and to tell him how proud she had been of him. This kind of support from another adult may have a deep impact on your child. They need role models in their lives, in addition to their parents, who will encourage them in their faith, understand their problems, and help guide them along life's way.

Have other adults into your home frequently, and participate in outings with other families. Promote conversation between your children and other adults, and pray for God to bring mentors of this type into the lives of your children. Be willing to be that other adult in someone else's child's life. This is one way we support each other in the body of Christ.

We never arrive at being "perfect parents." Teenagers make us realize in new ways how imperfect we are. Learning to parent takes a lifetime. We make many mistakes, but there is no mistake God cannot rectify, no crisis he cannot redeem, "for nothing is impossible with God" (Luke 1:37). Remember, he is using our teens to help *us* mature into the men and women he has created us to be.

QUESTIONS FOR REFLECTION

1. What fears do you have about raising teenagers?
2. How is the culture you are living in impacting your expectations and values for your children? For example, is there a particular issue concerning a child in which you are being more influenced by the culture around you than by godly wisdom?
3. What steps can you take during this season to keep communication healthy with your children?
4. Do you know an older couple who have good relationships with their children and whose children have a vital faith? Would you seek their wisdom during this season?

---

*Now to him who is able to do immeasurably more than all we ask
or imagine, according to his power that is at work within us,
to him be glory in the church and in Christ Jesus throughout
all generations, for ever and ever! Amen.*

Ephesians 3:20–21

13

Preparing Your Child
for Independence
John III with Siblings

Six o'clock A.M. has always been a surprisingly active time in our home. My earliest memories of that hour stretch back over many years. Although I was hard-pressed to leave the warmth of my bed on weekday mornings, Saturdays were altogether different. With machine-like precision I would be up and headed for the television in time for my favorite cartoons to begin. As I padded quietly downstairs and along the ground-floor corridor, I would see a familiar glow emanating from my father's study at the end of the hallway. En route to the television I would pause for a glimpse at my father's praying form, bent intently over notebooks and photographs of family, friends, and missionaries.

Years passed, and Saturday became the one day of the week on which I wasn't forced awake regularly at 6:00 A.M. School started early, and in order to move five children through the rigors of a school-day morning, an early start was required. On my way to a shower in the basement, I saw that same familiar glow around Dad's partially open study door. Inside I would see his silently praying form.

Not long after 6:00 A.M. in London, the ambitious businessman is already on his way to work in "the city." This hour sees me struggle out of bed, into the shower, past the kitchen for a cup of tea, and to my desk, from which glows the familiar light of a lamp, silhouetting a young man bent over Bible and notebook, praying like his dad.

It is difficult to know the right formula for how to raise a child to follow Christ once he reaches adulthood. Faithful parents throughout the biblical narrative sometimes succeeded and sometimes failed miserably. When God's grace seems to be given at random, is there anything parents can do to instill in their children a right love for their Creator and Redeemer?

Of course, there are many things a parent can do. But perhaps the greatest gifts a parent can give a child are a love for God's Word and a passion for prayer. Developing one's own faith, independent from one's parents', is *the* significant stepping-stone for children on the way to mature, independent adulthood. This is done in many little ways, but the best is through personal example. There is no mistake that my earliest memories of my father are of his praying form silhouetted by the light on his desk. It was his example, and that of my mother, as they daily went about the core disciplines of the faith, that bore in me the firstfruits of my own independent life as a Christian.

INDEPENDENCE STARTS EARLY

For the Yates kids, independence began when we were old enough to reach the kitchen counter. With five of us running around, it would be an understatement to say that Mom had her hands full during the day. Early morning was especially difficult. Between helping one child find her shoes and another his homework, while simultaneously laying out breakfast, there was little time left to prepare school lunches. So, as soon as we could be trusted with a butter knife and a glass jar of peanut butter, we were on our own for making lunch.

We started making our own lunches at the age when almost all the other kids at school still had lunches made for them. Although they often had tidier brown bags and perfectly sliced sandwiches, I distinctly remember a sort of pride in my peanut-butter-stained bag and jelly-dripping sandwich. I didn't need someone to make my lunch for me. I could do it on my own. It's a simple illustration, and one already used in this book, but it bears repeating as it demonstrates several of the principles involved in preparing children for independence.

Preparing your children for eventual independence begins at an early age. As kids grow and are able to take on responsibilities, they should not only be allowed, but encouraged, to do so. Early lessons in independence go a long way toward bearing fruit when children are eventually on their own. Perhaps a better, yet similar, example is cooking dinner. It is a well-known fact in our family that Mom is not a great cook. A woman of immeasurable gifts and abilities, she lacks instinct in the kitchen. As a result, she would often hand over responsibility for dinner to one of the kids when we were teenagers. As finicky teenagers this was often a welcome opportunity to cook what we were willing to eat. It was also, unbeknownst to us at the time, training for adulthood. Now, when I have small dinner parties at my apartment in London, friends are constantly surprised that I can cook—and I don't even have a microwave!

Preparing a child for independence starts with the sharing of responsibility and the expectation that he will be responsible and trustworthy. For although trust is ultimately earned, it first has to be given. A child who has been trusted and has over time proved himself to be trustworthy will be much better able to make wise decisions once he is on his own. It will also be much easier for his parents to let him go.

INCREASING SUPPORT

In the chapter on discipline two important principles were discussed: support and control. A home where there is high support and high control from an early age was shown to be the most effective in terms of encouraging obedience and developing self-discipline. As children come into their late teen years, however, control will gradually diminish in appropriate ways. This comes to a climax of sorts when a child leaves home, often for college or university, sometimes to a full-time job.

Some children will show no desire or inclination to leave home and establish their independence. This is fine up to a point. When a child has reached adulthood and is capable of independent life, it is unhealthy for him to stay at home depending on his parents' support. In this situation it may be necessary for parents to give him a gentle push out the door and into independence. The longer a child stays at home when he is capable of independence, the more he will become psychologically dependent on his parents, and the more difficult it will be for him ultimately to leave.

More often than not, however, young people are far more eager to leave home than their parents are to see them go. At this point, for good or ill, physical control over one's children becomes impossible. Options left for a concerned parent are threefold. You could try to exert long-distance control through phone calls, emails, and letters; you could gratefully wash your hands of the responsibility of exercising any control at all; or you could seek to redefine what sort of control, in conjunction with support, is now appropriate. This third option, though the hardest, is clearly the best.

When children leave home for college or elsewhere, one of the greatest thrills for them is the freedom that comes with independence. Don't ruin this! Perhaps one of the worst things parents can do is to call their child during his or her first night at college. A parent who tries to exercise excessive control from long distance succeeds only in egging a child on to sever himself more completely from that control. Yet a parent who visibly washes her hands of any control over her child's life shows a lack of care. Where is the balance to be found?

Often the best place to start is by turning up levels of support. When your ability to control is limited, offering wise support is an excellent alternative. Be interested in what your child is doing, ask about his new friends, ask about his classes or work. Don't ask what time he goes to bed each night and whether he is eating healthily. Whether your child has departed for college or simply moved to his own apartment in another part of the city and taken his first job, you can be assured that he is staying up too late and not eating his vegetables! This is regrettable but normal.

One of the best ways my parents showed support for me was by writing periodic letters or sending brief notes in the mail. My mother would often write a few words on a Post-it note when forwarding mail from home. I still have several of these "love notes" today. Getting mail, any mail, is a great thing; and to a young person sensitive about his or her independence, it is less intrusive than a phone call. A letter takes more energy than a phone call and more time than an email. Kids know this. If a mother has taken the time to write even a short note to her daughter, it communicates that she cares and desires to be involved in her life in a way that is neither intrusive on the one hand nor too far removed on the other. Regular phone calls marked by nagging questions about social life, sleeping and eating habits don't—they communicate to your nineteen-year-old son that you do not trust him. In these areas, of course, you probably shouldn't trust him, but he'll manage to survive on limited sleep and will eventually learn to like broccoli—maybe.

ACCEPTABLE CONTROL

"Increased support is a good idea," a concerned parent might concede, "but am I supposed to abdicate all control when my daughter is off on her own?" No. There will still be situations where the exercise of control is not only possible but necessary. With the many temptations that come with independence, young people are bound to mess up in some way. Unwise behavior shouldn't be condoned, but neither should it be dwelt on. Wise parents will let a child know how they feel and leave it at that without nagging.

Showing a disregard for the law or for important family principles, however, is unacceptable. When a child has been out drinking irresponsibly or illegally, or has willfully broken a university policy or law, something must be done. In situations like this parents should not be afraid to take a stand. Early independence is often a time of pushing one's limits. Sometimes young people push too hard and before they know it have gone over the edge. For the recently launched young adult, this is a time of testing oneself but also of testing one's parents' levels of tolerance.

Thus, it is important for parents to take a stand when pushed. Young adults will need boundaries set for them if they fail to set their own. If a student willfully goes against an established family policy and her father fails to take a stand, she will detect a weakness and may lose respect for her father, which may lead to further exploitation of that weakness. For example, if a parent fails to condemn a night of underage drinking, he fails to stand up for what he believes. By not condemning his child's action, he is a party to it through his own unwillingness to stand up for what he believes.

One area where parents will most certainly be challenged and will need to be firm is money. University students especially will never have enough and will always want more. Most will come to Mom and Dad when they run out. This is one of the simple rules of early independence. And this is one area where it is okay for parents to be unpopular. Students living away from home won't naturally balance their checkbook or pay off a new credit card every month. Laying down guidelines before a child goes off to college is the best way to forestall major problems, but a parent shouldn't hesitate to get involved if problems do arise.

Discerning which issues demand taking a stand is difficult. Loosening one's control often means letting children learn things the hard way. It may mean allowing your child to walk into mistakes that could have been avoided, in order for them to learn the necessary lesson. I had a friend in college who must have given his mother fits as a result of persistent irresponsibility. During our first semester he missed one early morning class so many times that he came within one absence of failing. His eventual solution for the last few weeks of the semester was to sleep in the classroom the night before class so he would be there the following morning. This particular friend spent his first few years failing at good time management but eventually learned his lesson the hard way. He is now in the military and gets up punctually at 4:30 every morning. There is hope for all of us!

In my friend's situation a nagging mother may have pushed him over the edge. On the other hand, if his parents had shown no regard for his class attendance, he probably would have failed. His parents' promise to deal with him harshly spurred him on to the extreme action necessary to pass his class. His parents drew a line and stood by it. Their ability to do so was helped greatly by the ongoing involvement they had in his life at college through letter writing, sending "care packages," and generally showing interest in his life. By being involved, though at a respectful distance, and showing they cared, they earned the right to step in when more than support was necessary.

Perhaps a good maxim to follow is: Let young adults make mistakes as long as they continue to learn from them. When mistakes fail to become lessons learned or pose a clear danger to their livelihood, it is time to intervene.

Visiting Home

Perhaps the greatest test of the parent-child relationship after young people have left for college or have left to live on their own is when they return home to visit. What should be a joyful reunion often ends in disappointment, with parents and child surprised at what is happening.

The story of the wedding at Cana in Galilee, told to us in John 2, gives a little insight into Jesus' interaction with his mother not long after he had left home and established his independence. It seems that Joseph, Jesus' father, had died while he was still young. Being the oldest child, Jesus would have had to carry a lot of responsibility for the care of the family. His mother, Mary, would have depended on him heavily. Now, however, he was on his own. He had begun teaching and had accumulated a small group of followers. They were all invited to a wedding in Cana with which his mother had some involvement. When the wedding party ran out of wine, Mary headed straight for Jesus. And, as is often the case when young adults return home, Jesus' mother began giving directions.

"They have no more wine," she said simply, with the clear implication that Jesus was to do something about it.

Being an independent man, Jesus didn't have to meet her request, nor, for good reason, did he want to. He replied, "Dear woman, why do you involve me? My time has not yet come." Mary, a strong-minded widow used to doing things as she wished, wouldn't take no for an answer. Turning to the servants, she said, "Do whatever he tells you."

Jesus had a choice to make. Either he could honor his mother and reveal himself through miraculously turning water into wine, or he could legitimately refuse, delaying the time at which his miraculous powers would be publicly recognized. Although the decision was his, and he did not have to obey his mother, he did. He turned water into wine, revealing his glory, and his disciples put their faith in him.

My first visit home wasn't quite so memorable. Being only two hours away, I decided to make the journey one weekend for some much needed rest and non-dining hall food. I was looking forward to being pampered and treated like a guest. Little did I know what was in store for me.

Not only was I not treated like a guest, but I had to do chores that weekend. I also had a curfew and was asked to wash the dishes after dinner the first night I was back. It was as if I'd never left! Of course, for my

169

parents this must have seemed the case. I'd only been away for just over a month, and *they* certainly hadn't changed in that time. I, on the other hand, had just spent a whole month living on my own in a new place, following my own set of rules, and enjoying the freedom of college. At the time it seemed my parents clearly had no regard for my newfound independence!

It was a miserable weekend. I left on Sunday afternoon annoyed with my parents for being themselves and angry with myself for responding like a spoiled toddler. How should I have acted differently? Was I wrong to expect them to treat me differently? What was the right balance?

Home can be a stifling place for an independent young adult. Parents will need to recognize this even if they don't understand why. Sometimes just the fact of being at home creates a sense of resentment toward parents' supposed desire to curtail one's freedom. As a result, young people returning home from college will often want little to do with their parents. This is natural, and in these situations it is only right to give them space. Be willing to have your attempts at being involved or showing concern pushed aside. On these occasions, parents need to give their kids space without abandoning them. It is another example of the need for increased support and slackened control.

Over the course of time my parents and I managed to find a working balance. Time at home was not completely free from tension, but they began to understand my need for independence better, and I came to appreciate the fact that home was still theirs to run as they saw fit. Their control began to slacken as I demonstrated responsibility. Curfews were eventually rescinded, and a more relaxed atmosphere on both sides prevailed. Conveniently, this was about the same time I decided I didn't like staying out much after midnight anyway!

BUILDING A FRIENDSHIP

Although visits home may be difficult at times, they are also good times for building a friendship with a child on the verge of adulthood. This is best done away from the house itself, on neutral ground. Ask your kids to do fun things with you. If you share a sport in common, play together. One of my favorite things to do at home is play tennis (mixed doubles) with my mother and a few of her friends.

One of the greatest gifts parents can give a young adult child is the gift of their friends. I have had more fun than I ever thought possible with my parents' friends. As a young adult nothing is more reaffirming than being treated as a peer by your parents' friends. Being invited to join conversations, being asked your opinion, and being treated like an adult all go a long way toward helping a young adult mature to the point where he recognizes the responsibilities that come with the honor of such a claim.

Building a deep friendship with an adult child is the eventual reward that follows the often painful process of their increasing independence. It begins with the gradual relinquishing of control amid continuing support. And it further develops as you become peers. In this sense parenthood becomes a walking alongside rather than a pulling from the front or pushing from behind. I think the greatest thrill in parenting must be when a child has passed through the storms of teenage struggle and the increased distance of the springtime of independence and returns home as a friend and peer.

Of course, such a friendship will not grow and deepen without effort. As children grow up, more issues arise that will need to be addressed. As they marry, further issues of independence, not to mention balance between in-laws, will come up, and the relationship will have to grow and adjust accordingly.

One natural way to help friendship with adult children grow deeper is to let them be involved in the decision making and dreaming that go on in midlife and later. As you have sought to be involved in their lives, seek to involve them in yours. By asking advice and seeking the input of their children, parents demonstrate high levels of trust and respect— qualities young adults want most to possess. One easy way to do this is by asking your children—of all ages—to pray for you. Sharing prayer requests and enlisting their prayer support communicates respect that all children hunger for.

Another way for parents to show continuing support and interest in the lives of their adult children is to visit them. Far too often parents unthinkingly expect their children to come home and visit them during vacations, forgetting that they now have homes of their own. When a young adult's vacations are entirely taken up with going home, they become limited in what they are able to do and gradually resent it. My parents recently came to visit me in London. They took ten days to see me and to explore the English countryside. The fact that they came all the way to England to spend time with me and to see me in my natural habitat meant a great deal. It showed not only that they cared for me, but that they were interested in what I was doing, in my friends, and in the city in which I live.

This time of transition from dependence to independence can be stressful for both children and parents. Parents will often feel like ignored coaches standing on the sidelines shouting themselves hoarse only to be ignored by the players on the field. For kids it often feels like having a persistent backseat driver distracting you as you negotiate new and often treacherous roads. Thankfully, this time of stress and miscommunication doesn't last forever. As a child becomes more thoroughly independent, and as parents let go more completely of control, the opportunity for deep peer friendships arises. With continued support and involvement in each other's lives, the path is paved for these friendships to form. All it takes is a little work, some unavoidable misunderstanding thrown in for good measure, and a desire for deep, godly friendship to mark your adult lives together.

QUESTIONS FOR REFLECTION

1. What was it like for you as a young adult when you first left home? How did your parents handle this time in your life? What mistakes did they make? What did they do right?
2. What do you think will be the greatest challenge for you when your children leave home? What will be the greatest challenge for them?
3. How can you and your mate be preparing for this time now?
4. What things might you be praying for now regarding this period of change and adjustment for you and your children?

Trust in the LORD *with all your heart*
and lean not on your own understanding;
in all your ways acknowledge him,
and he will make your paths straight.

Proverbs 3:5–6

14

Praying for Your Family
John

In the Old Testament Book of Judges (chapter 17), there is a rather strange story about a man named Micah. As an older man Micah became suddenly aware of his own and his family's spiritual neediness. He confessed his sins to the rest of his family and then he went out and hired a man to become the family priest. He found a young priest and said basically: "Move into our family. I appoint you to be priest and father to me and my family. I know now that everything is going to go well with us."

But things did not go well. It is significant that Micah didn't believe he was adequate to provide spiritually for his family, so he hired a "professional" to meet the spiritual needs of his home. Micah eventually realized that he had been mistaken about this, for his decision had drastic consequences, including great loss, trickery, idol worship, and tragedy. God has appointed *us* to be priests in our own homes.

Throughout this book we have stressed the need for us as parents to be praying for our family members as well as for ourselves. This is a big responsibility and an even bigger privilege. Parents who love their own family will pray for them. But for many prayer doesn't come easily. In spite of this, we need to embrace our responsibility, for it is at the heart of effective parenting. We refer to this as a part of the parents' priestly role in the home.

Prayer can be awkward and difficult. A friend of mine says learning to pray is like going for a jog after a hurricane. The trees and bushes are uprooted, utility poles are blown down, and there's water everywhere. You try to run around all the obstacles but just keep getting caught up short, having to stop or turn around and find another way. For a lot of us praying is like that. Following are several suggestions that may be helpful to you as you learn to pray for your family.

ESTABLISH A TIME AND A PLACE

The apostle Paul says that we should pray at all times, but we will never learn to pray at all times unless we learn to pray at certain times. So establish a time and attempt to preserve that time every day. Then decide on a place where you can be still and quiet without interruptions. Realize that God is in that place, wherever it is, and therefore it is a holy place. God says, "Be still, and know that I am God" (Ps. 46:10). You can do that in the car, or in the living room, or in the backyard. We all have demanding schedules and responsibilities. I hardly know anyone, whatever their job, who is not busy. But if you are too busy to pray, you are simply too busy.

My own habit for years has been to set aside time early in the morning. I arise before the rest of the family, because that is easier for me. I do my exercises, shave, take a shower, then go to the kitchen and make a steaming cup of coffee. I take that to my little room, shut the door, and then I'm ready to meet with the Almighty.

BEGIN WITH GRATITUDE

Begin by thanking God. Take a moment or two to look back over the past few days and give God thanks for the blessings that come to your mind. If you begin the day with thankfulness, it will give you a sense of joy and peace. We have a pet golden retriever whose name is Bishop. I have frequently observed how he begins his own day. He arises slowly and stretches himself carefully. He looks up at the sky and then rolls over and rubs his back, holding his paws up into the air as though praying to his Creator! He is so full of joy just to be alive. One can have many problems and yet still find joy in simply being alive if he begins with gratitude and thanksgiving.

EXAMINE THE DAY PAST

Think over the past twenty-four hours and ask God to help you remember what happened. What experiences did you have? With whom did you meet? How did you feel? Is there sin you need to confess? What did you learn? Do you need to make note of something you learned to reaffirm it in your mind? What blessings occurred? What failures? Think back through the last day, review it, and take to God anything you think of that is significant, asking him to help you profit from yesterday.

FOCUS ON TODAY

Consider today's concerns. You might think about the people you're going to be with or the responsibilities that are waiting for you when you leave this quiet place. Maybe you will pull out your daily calendar and look at appointments or plans. Perhaps you will recall problems or things about which you are uncertain. Pray about these things one by one, asking God to help you to be adequate for the challenges you face during the day. Ask him to fill you with his Holy Spirit and make you joyful, to fill you with peace, to make you adequate for the day. Once you have taken time for these things, you are ready for intercession on behalf of loved ones.

PRAYING FOR YOUR FAMILY

A Canaanite woman who had a demon-possessed daughter once approached Jesus on her daughter's behalf. She came to Jesus at a time when he was trying to have a little privacy. He seemed to ignore her. Perhaps he was seeking to teach his disciples something at that moment. She, however, persisted in imploring him. Finally, in his own time, he responded by meeting the little girl's need. This woman shows us a good deal about praying for our family. She comes to God through Christ, and so must we, for he is our mediator. She acknowledges her need, coming in humility, and she tells Jesus specifically what her needs are. She makes careful, clear requests. Finally, she is persistent. She does not lose heart. She is a good model for us as praying parents.

A wise parent realizes three things early on about children. First, you don't need to do for your children what they can do for themselves. Second, loving parents try to provide for the needs of their children as well as they possibly can. This doesn't mean you give them everything they want. It does mean, however, that the things they can't do for themselves you do to the best of your ability for them. Third, there are many things parents can't do for their child, and this is where prayer is so important. You ask God to do for them the things you would like to be able to do but can't do for them. For instance, you can train your child to know the difference between right and wrong, but you can't force your child to do what is right.

It helps when praying for loved ones to envision them before Jesus Christ. Jesus was unfailingly compassionate when people came to him with needs. So, when I pray for my loved ones, I try to envision them coming to the Lord, either kneeling before him or standing or sitting, and I picture him reaching out to them. I ask myself, "What would he say to them? What would he want to do in their lives?" Then I ask him to do those things in their lives. As you pray for family and friends, bring them one by one before the Lord, thanking him for their good qualities and interceding on behalf of their needs.

I, like many others, have learned to use a little prayer notebook in which I keep pictures of family members and friends and jot down particular needs. I try to pray for everyone in my family every day as best I can—my children, my wife, my mother, my mother-in-law, my brothers, my sisters—mentioning any particular needs they are facing that day.

In addition to these prayers, each day of the week I set aside a little time to pray for a particular member of the family more extensively. For instance, on Monday I pray particularly for my oldest daughter and her family. Perhaps they are in the midst of making a major decision and need wisdom. Or maybe the baby has been keeping them up at night and they need strength. On Wednesday I pray for my second son, taking more time to pray specifically for particular needs that I don't take the time to pray for every day. I may pray about his long-range career choices and ask God to give me particular insight into how I can help him to grow in discernment. In a case such as this, I might spend several minutes prayerfully pondering this, making notes as to ideas and possible actions to be taken. Perhaps I would take time to pray more specifically for students in a class he is teaching.

You may be saying to yourself, "I'm not sure I know how to pray. I'm not sure I know what's the right thing to pray for. Maybe I shouldn't bother God with this." Dear friend, if it is a concern to you, then it is a concern to God. If it is a concern to your child, it is a concern to God. If you're not absolutely sure you should be asking God for something, just ask yourself, "Is this something Christ would like to see happen? Would Christ sign his name to this prayer I'm praying?" That's what Jesus meant when he said, "You may ask me for anything in my name, and I will do it" (John 14:14). Pray a prayer you believe he would agree with and be persistent. The Canaanite woman had to ask and keep on asking, and so will we. In every stage of life your family members and friends have needs for which they need you to intercede on their behalf.

On occasion I've looked through a number of my prayer notebooks to be reminded of how I've prayed for a specific child. I might observe, for instance, that when this child was about two years old, I was praying for her to know that her mom and dad loved her, that she would begin to learn Bible stories, and that she would begin to learn how to pray and give her life to God. A year or so later my notes show that I was praying she would come to love her new little brother. I prayed that she wouldn't hear or see the ugly things of the world until she was old enough. When she was four I spent four months praying that she would have a better appetite at mealtimes. The prayer was crossed through and had double checks at the end of it, which meant that eventually I saw that prayer answered. When she was five I was praying for her manners to improve. When she was six I was asking that she would develop more of a curious nature and not be too inhibited. When she was seven I was asking that God would guide us to books that we could read together that would help her mature and understand things that she needed to understand. When she was twelve I was praying that she would excel in her tennis and know how proud her parents were of her. When she was seventeen I was praying for her college finances to work out and for guidance for her summer plans that year. When she was nineteen I was praying for greater discernment for her, and for excellent teachers in college who would be outstanding models for her, and that she would have a strong and supportive relationship with a friend named Heidi. My notes go on and on. Now I'm praying for her and her husband, for their daughter Caroline, and for the second child, Will.

As I look over these briefly written notes compiled over the last thirty years, I'm amazed and overwhelmed at the goodness of God in answering so many prayers for my daughter with a yes. I'm glad he didn't answer them all with a yes, because they weren't all wise requests. Sometimes he answered with a no. Sometimes he said, "You are going to have to wait on that one." This is not just a record of her life, it's a record of God's faithfulness in taking care of her.

I began praying for each of our children when they were conceived. Then when we brought them home from the hospital, my wife and I laid them on the bed, got on our knees, and thanked God together for each of these children, dedicating them to him for his purposes and asking for his help. I began the habit, as soon as the first one came home from the hospital, of slipping into their rooms at night as they were going to sleep and putting my hand on their heads and asking God's blessing on them. These are different ways in which we try to be priests to our children.

In his second letter to Timothy, Paul wrote, "I have been reminded of your sincere faith, which first lived in your grandmother Lois and in your mother Eunice and, I am persuaded, now lives in you also" (1:5). In other words, Timothy's grandmother's faith had been passed on to him. This reminds us not just to pray for this generation, but to pray down the generations, for our children, for their children, their children's children, and their mates. We have had praying grandmothers on both sides of our family, and we are certain that one of the reasons our lives have been so blessed is that they prayed down the generations for us. One man I know, an outstanding Christian leader in the United States, recalled that his great-grandfather had begun years ago praying regularly for the next four generations that each one would end up loving God and serving him in their vocations. He realized one day that his children were the end of that prayer chain, and he thought, "I had better pick up where Granddad left off." He began to use Fridays as a day of fasting and prayer for the next several generations.

From time to time a contrast has been drawn between two families in New England, one of whom had a praying patriarch, the other who didn't. The first was a pastor known to have at least 929 descendants. At least 430 were ministers. There were 86 university professors, 13 university presidents, 75 authors, 7 U.S. congressmen, and 1 vice president of the United States. This praying patriarch was Jonathan Edwards, a man who acted as a priest for his family.

The other man was a contemporary of Edwards. He spent a good deal of his life in prison and wasn't known to be a believer. He didn't take his children to church even when they asked him to. We know that he had at least 1,026 descendants. Of his family members, 300 were sent to prison for an average of thirteen years. Another 190 were public prostitutes. Some 680 were admitted alcoholics. His family had cost the state hundreds of thousands of dollars (today it would be millions). Here is an example of a radically dysfunctional family. Consider how this family line might have been different had there been more prayer.

We can make a difference in the future generations if we start praying now. Prayer isn't man's idea. God tells us to pray. Jesus, the very Son of God, prayed constantly. Prayer is at the heart of friendship with God, and prayer for our families is a top priority.

QUESTIONS FOR REFLECTION

1. Consider and write out the needs of each member of your family in five areas of growth: spiritual, physical, mental, emotional, and social.
2. Based on the above, write a prayer that you will use for the coming year for each member of your family.

In the morning, O LORD, you hear my voice;
in the morning I lay my requests before you
and wait in expectation.

Psalm 5:3

Notes

Chapter 2: Three Essential Commitments for Building the Christian Home

1. David Blankenhorn, *Fatherless America* (New York: Harper Perennial, 1995).

Chapter 3: Establishing a Strong Marriage

1. J. I. Packer, *Knowing God* (Downers Grove, Ill.: InterVarsity, 1973), 29.

2. From John Yates, *For the Life of the Family* (Wilton, Conn.: Morehouse-Barlowe, 1984), 13.

3. Ibid., 32.

4. Ibid., 31.

Chapter 5: The First Child

1. Frank Minirth, Frank Newman, and Paul Warren, *The Father Book: An Instruction Manual* (Nashville: Thomas Nelson, 1996).

Chapter 6: Motherhood

1. See our book *What Really Matters at Home: Eight Crucial Elements for Building Character in Your Family* (Dallas: Word, 1992).

Chapter 7: Fatherhood

1. David Blankenhorn, *Washington Post,* 21 August 1998, A3.

2. James C. Dobson, *What Wives Wish Their Husbands Knew about Women* (Wheaton: Tyndale House, 1975).

Chapter 9: Building Christian Character

1. You may wish to refer to Susan Alexander Yates, *And Then I Had Kids,* (Grand Rapids: Baker, 2002) which focuses more thoroughly on these questions.

John Yates is rector of The Falls Church (Episcopal) in Falls Church, Virginia. **Susan Yates** has written several books and is a frequent guest on *FamilyLife Today* and other national radio programs. They are popular speakers at marriage and family conferences around the country. Their five children (and their spouses) have joined them in writing this book about the family.

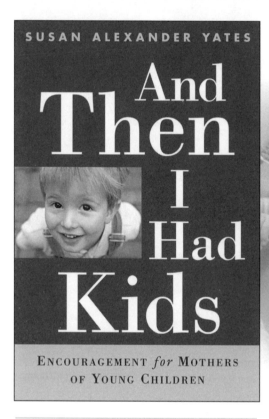

SUSAN ALEXANDER YATES

And
Then
I
Had
Kids

ENCOURAGEMENT *for* MOTHERS
OF YOUNG CHILDREN

AND THEN I HAD KIDS
Encouragement for Mothers of Young Children
BY SUSAN ALEXANDER YATES

This book is ideal for mothers of children
ages eight and under. It makes a great gift for
new or overwhelmed moms who wonder,
"Does anyone else feel like this?" Chapters
include "Maintaining a Positive Self-Image,"
"Solving the Discipline Dilemma,"
"Establishing Priorities That Work," "Finding
Good Role Models," "Becoming a Best Friend
in Marriage," and many others. Questions at
the end of each chapter make this perfect for
a moms' study group.

And Then I Had Teenagers

Encouragement for Parents of Teens and Preteens
By Susan Alexander Yates

"You just don't understand!" "But all my friends get to . . ."
"Why can't you trust me?" "I'm not sure I believe . . ."
We've all heard similar phrases. If your kids are approaching the teen years or looking at colleges, this book is for you. It examines ten challenges for parents of teens or preteens and provides many practical solutions that will enable this season to be enjoyed, not merely endured. The book offers help for parents facing normal teen issues as well as painful crises. End-of-chapter questions make this a good resource for small groups.

JOHN & SUSAN YATES

Character Matters!

Raising Kids with Values That Last

CHARACTER MATTERS!
Raising Kids with Values That Last
BY JOHN AND SUSAN YATES

If you want to help your kids develop strong character, this book is for you! It takes eight character traits—including integrity, a servant's heart, a teachable spirit, and courage—and explains how to instill them in children. The Yateses use stories and practical examples to show how character can be purposefully cultivated through the normal, daily events in life. A complete leader's guide makes this book perfect for small groups, including single parents.

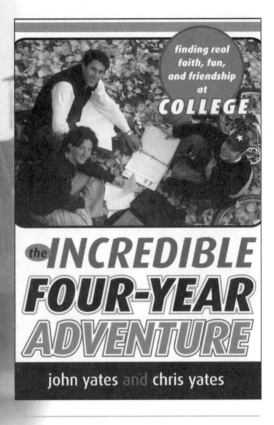

finding real
faith, fun,
and friendship
at
COLLEGE

the **INCREDIBLE**
FOUR-YEAR
ADVENTURE

john yates and chris yates

THE INCREDIBLE FOUR-YEAR ADVENTURE
Finding Real Faith, Fun, and Friendship at College
BY JOHN YATES AND CHRIS YATES

Written by two recent college graduates (and brothers!), this is a must read for juniors and seniors in high school and for any college student. The book discusses everything students are likely to encounter on a secular or Christian campus, including roommates, dating, choosing classes, finding a campus fellowship group, and fraternity/sorority rush. In addition, it offers strategies for holding on to your faith. End-of-chapter questions make this an excellent resource for a small group setting.

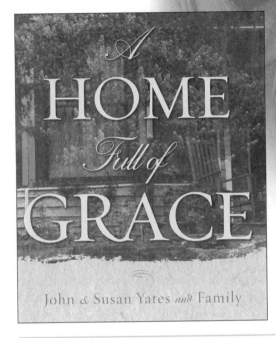

A Home Full of Grace
By John and Susan Yates and Family

Written by the entire Yates family, *A Home Full of Grace* incorporates portions of *Building a Home Full of Grace* into a beautifully designed gift book. It covers everything from marriage to the time children leave home. Topics include what it means to be a Christian family, seasons of family life, the first child, the teen years, cultivating faith, and praying for family members. It makes a lovely gift for a new believer or for weddings, anniversaries, holidays, and birthdays.